D0152727

Sir George ETHEREGE

a reference guide

A
Reference
Guide
to
Literature

Arthur J. Weitzman
Editor

Sir George ETHEREGE
a reference guide

DAVID D. MANN

G.K.HALL &CO.

70 LINCOLN STREET, BOSTON, MASS.

Library of Congress Cataloging in Publication Data

Mann, David D.
  Sir George Etherege : a reference guide.

  Bibliography:
  Includes index.
  1. Etherege, George, Sir, 1635?-1691—Bibliography.
I.   Title.
Z8273.47.M36   [PR3432]   016.822′4   81-4808
ISBN 0-8161-8171-3   AACR2

This publication is printed on permanent/durable acid-free paper
MANUFACTURED IN THE UNITED STATES OF AMERICA

For my brother and sisters--
        Loftin Mann
        Betty Cooper
        Dorothy Cameron
        Jeannette Stewart

Contents

The Author

David Douglas Mann (Ph.D., Indiana University, 1969) has compiled a
Concordance to the Plays of William Congreve (Cornell University
Press, 1973) and an edition of the Plays of Theophilus and Susanah
Cibber (Garland, 1981). Besides his interest in Restoration and
Eighteenth-Century drama, he has written on Robert Louis Stevenson
(with W. H. Hardesty), William Butler Yeats, John Crowe Ramsom, and
detective fiction. From 1978 to 1980, Mann taught at the Miami
University European Center, Luxembourg and at the Centre Universit-
aire, Luxembourg. During these years in Europe, he spent his summers
working at the Bodelian Library, Oxford, England, where much of
George Etherege: A Reference Guide was compiled.

Mann is Professor of English at Miami University, Oxford, Ohio,
where he also serves as Assistant Director of Graduate Studies.

Etherege's Major Works
and
Dates of First Publication

Abbreviations

ARS =   Augustan Reprint Society. Los Angeles: W. A. Clark
            Memorial Library. Up to volume 200 by 1980.

DA =   Dissertation Abstracts, 1938-69.

DAI =   Dissertation Abstracts International, 1969- .

McNamee = McNamee, Lawrence F., comp. Dissertations in English and
          American Literature: Theses Accepted by American, British
          and German Universities, 1865-1964. New York: R. R.
          Bowker, 1968. Supplement One, 1964-68. New York: R. R.
          Bowker, 1969. Supplement Two, 1968-72. New York: R. R.
          Bowker, 1973. See Introduction, pp. xiv.

POAS =   Poems on Affairs of State. See 1963.B3 for modern edition.

RECTR =   Restoration and Eighteenth-Century Theatre Research.
            1961.

TLS =   Times Literary Supplement (London).

Wing =   Wing, Donald G. A Short-Title Catalogue of Books Printed
            in England, Scotland, Ireland, Wales, and British America,
            and of English Books Printed in Other Countries, 1641-1700.
            3 vols. New York: Columbia University Press, 1945-51.
            Vol. 1, 2nd. ed., New York: Modern Language Association,
            1972. Vols. 2 & 3 of 2d. ed. in preparation.

W&M =   Woodward, Gertrude L., and McManaway, James G. A Check
            List of English Plays, 1641-1700. Chicago: Newberry
            Library, 1945.

Introduction

This bibliography is intended for scholars, graduate students, and advanced undergraduates who wish to make a study of the works of Sir George Etherege, poet and playwright of the seventeenth century, and who wish to see the trends of the criticism on his work. Because of the slender amount of primary material--three plays, about forty poems, and some four-hundred letters--I have been as inclusive as possible. Hence the user of this bibliography will find peripheral matter cited as well as important books and articles. In my approach I tried to be as complete as possible by tracking down sources cited in footnotes, by checking bibliographies in books and dissertations, and by seeking advice from fellow Etheregeans (especially Frederick Bracher, Arthur Huseboe, and Robert Hume). I then attempted to locate and read every book and article; those I was unable to obtain, I have marked with an asterisk and noted my source. Using this method, I aimed at providing pointed and fresh annotations, quoting the author wherever I could. In every case, I have tried to be as objective as possible in my annotations, but I did feel it necessary to note factual errors, incomplete details, and observed biases; in some cases I have referred the researcher to contrasting views in other books and essays cited in this bibliography. In short, I have had in mind from the first a bibliography that would be useful to the researcher.

Much of the criticism of Etherege is contained in pieces on Restoration comedy and may well include remarks on other dramatists of the age--Dryden, Wycherley, Congreve, Vanbrugh, Farquhar, Cibber, or Steele. Although I have focused the annotations on the critical reception and reputation of Etherege's work over the past three-hundred years, I expect that those interested in Restoration drama will find the annotations useful in getting a broader view of the genre and in seeing Etherege's place in this tradition of English theatre.

Bibliographical Organization

This Reference Guide is arranged chronologically from 1664 to 1978. In addition, I have included the pieces on Etherege I have run across from 1979 and 1980. Under each year, there are two kinds of entries: Category A contains books and dissertations dealing entirely or mainly with Etherege and cites editions of the plays (printed singly or in anthologies). Category B includes secondary matter that treats Etherege's work (along with other writers of Restoration comedy) or that comments on his work in a significant way. In Category B are cited, then, portions of books or dissertations, essays, articles, and major reviews. Within these categories, I have made the following arrangements:

Category A: When listing Etherege's work printed in a given year, I have arranged the titles alphabetically. In the case of several reprints of the same play within a year, these are listed alphabetically by the title of the collection containing Etherege's play.

Category B: The secondary works, I have listed alphabetically by author within each year. If no author is given in the work, I provide the presumed author in square brackets, or indicate anonymous authorship by ANON. Dissertations with titles that suggest that Etherege's work may be included and that I have not seen are asterisked and listed under the year completed, with the appropriate source mentioned.

Items not included: (a) While I have listed editions printed in Etherege's lifetime, I have not provided full descriptive bibliographical details: these can be found in Brett-Smith's edition (1927.A1), pp. xciii–cviii. Some textual information about reprinted plays is given, though no wholesale collation was attempted. (b) Although I have consulted the best known bibliographies, such as the Cambridge Bibliography of English Literature, the New Cambridge Bibliography of English Literature, Donald F. Bond's Age of Dryden in the Goldentree Bibliography series, and Stratman's Restoration and Eighteenth-Century Theatre Research, 1900-1968; and the annual bibliographies appearing in PMLA, MHRA, PQ (since 1926), RECTR (since 1961), YWES, The Scriblerian, SEL, and Restoration (since 1977), I have not prepared individual entries for these lists. (c) I have also left the researcher to consult Thorpe (1963.A1) for early reprintings (as well as manuscripts) of Etherege's poetry. I have, however, included two songs that Sir George contributed to plays by Southerne (1684.B1) and Tate (1685.B1). (d) I have excluded unpublished M. A. theses. (e) I have not cited lists that can be found in major catalogues, such as the British Museum (now British Library) and the National Union Imprints. Occasionally, I will refer the reader to "McNamee," where dissertation titles can be found. Those dissertations I was unable to consult, and that might contain remarks on Etherege's work, I have culled from his entries in Dissertations in English and American Literature (New York: Bowker, 1968, with supplements in 1969 and 1974). Three brief bibliographical essays that I do list are Paine (1941.B1), Barnard (1975.B1), and Link (1976.B1). The results, then, are published in this Reference Guide, the first annotated bibliography to the works of and criticism on Sir George Etherege.

Biography
There are a good many isolated facts about the life of Sir George Etherege, but the difficulty of putting these facts together into a

coherent biography has proved an insurmountable problem. No full-scale biography of this courtier-author-diplomat exists. The best account of his life can be found in the introduction to The Letters, in which Frederick Bracher puts together most of the facts known about the man. Starting is not easy because we are not sure where Etherege was born. Maidenhead, various places in Oxfordshire, and Bermuda (his father was a shareholder in the Virginia and Bermuda Company) have been suggested. Nor do we know when he was born: dates from 1634 to 1637 have been proposed, but the summer of 1636 is Bracher's guess.

There is a tradition that he attended grammar school with Anthony à Wood at Thame, but no evidence has been found to support this claim. In 1654, he was apprenticed to George Gosnold, an attorney at Beaconsfield, and in 1659 went to Clement's Inn to read law. After the settlement of his grandfather's estate, Etherege may have traveled to France and Flanders. Bracher (1980.B1) concludes that "at some time during the period 1659-1663, Etherege apparently gave up serious study of the law in favor of his future role as man-about-town, playwright, and courtier."

After Etherege had written two plays and become involved with the court wits of the day, he was made a member of the Privy Council and appointed secretary to the English Ambassador to Turkey, Sir Daniel Harvey. He probably returned to London, via Paris, in 1671, and resumed his former life as a rakish courtier. By 1676, when Etherege wrote his last play, The Man of Mode, he was in the service of Mary of Modena, wife of the future James II. This connection may explain his dedication of the play to her. Bracher explains Etherege's next years thus: "between 1677 and 1679 Etherege was knighted and married, presumably in that order, since contemporary gossip had it that Etherege was given the knighthood so that he might marry his 'rich old widow.'" Contemporary scandalmongers said Etherege spent a good deal of time and a good deal of the widow's money at the gaming tables; this may explain why only a few occasional poems emerge from this period.

After the death of Charles II, James II offered Etherege the diplomatic post of English Resident to the Diet of the Holy Roman Empire. Etherege accepted the mission with alacrity, possible because of heavy gambling debts, and went off to Ratisbon via The Hague. Arriving in November 1685, Etherege set to work observing the sessions at the Diet and gathering information for the King. Barnard notes (1979.A1) that "by the end of his first year [Etherege] 'was practically a social outcast.'" But while he disliked the stuffy diplomatic parties, Etherege lead a private life much as he would have done in London. He cursed the "unhospitable" climate, and was often sick. Nevertheless, he kept up his biweekly correspondence to the Earl of Middleton in the foreign office. Furthermore, he carried on a steady correspondence with friends in England, including the Duke of Buckingham and John Dryden.

Introduction

When James II fled to France, Etherege went to Paris to join him.
Just exactly what his duties were is obscure, but Etherege did continue to write to his friends in England until September 1689. His
death is shrouded in as much mystery as his birth: it is likely that
he died in Paris (not in Ratisbon as some commentators have re-
ported), but again we cannot be sure. As for the date, guesses
range from 1690 to 1694. Moreover, we are not even sure what Etherege looked like, since no portrait of him seems to have survived.

The first attempt at a biography was undertaken by William Oldys
(1750.B2). In preparing an account for Biographia Britannica, Oldys
sought out people who knew Etherege, albeit from afar. There was
the old actor, John Bowman, who claims to have met the playwright,
and who retailed some anecdotes about him. Another informant was
Dean Lockier (see also Spence, 1966.B20), who provided the gossip
that Etherege died by falling down the stairs after a drunken party.
While Etherege was no doubt capable of this, Lockier was hardly in a
position to gain the knowledge firsthand. By the middle of the
eighteenth century, very few people had any interest in a rakish
Restoration playwright, who was a Jacobite at that.

After almost two centuries of neglect, Etherege did gain a sympathetic, though not always accurate, biographer in Edmund Gosse,
whose article in Cornhill Magazine (1881.B2) brought about a renewed
interest in Etherege the man. Gosse's use of Sir George's diplomatic correspondence from the Residency at Ratisbon, where he spent
more than three years as an observer of European affairs for James
II, provided a new insight into the man and his abilities. (The
letters were later edited and published as the Letterbook, 1928.A1.)
The dissertation of Vincenz Meindl (1901.A1) attempts to put together existing information on Etherege, but the biography (the first
part of the work) sheds no new light on the writer. When Bonamy
Dobrée published his short biography (1925.B1), he concentrated only
on the diplomatic years, relying heavily on the correspondence. H.
F. B. Brett-Smith corrects some of Dobrée's errors in a review (1927.
B1), and provides many more new biographical facts in his introduction to The Dramatic Works of Sir George Etherege (1927.A1). In the
same decade, Dorothy Foster collected a number of documents relating
to the playwright's life (1922.B1, B2, B3; 1927.B3; 1928.B3).

In preparing his edition of the Letters of Sir George Etherege
(1974.A1), Bracher uncovered yet more material (1967.B2, B3; 1969.
B1). Recently, Arthur Huseboe has discovered further facts about
the poet's mother (1975.B5), and Bracher has brought still more information to light about Etherege's time as a student at Clement's
Inn (1980.B1). Nevertheless, a full-scale biography of the playwright is lacking, although Huseboe is completing a biographical-
critical volume for the Twayne series on Etherege.

Work also remains to be done on Etherege's library. In the Letters, Bracher has supplied an appendix of the library of the play-

wright-turned-diplomat at his foreign post (see pp. 286-87 of 1974.
A1). Some of the books were left to the Scottish monastery at
Ratisbon (1864.B1; 1893.B3; 1906.B1) upon Etherege's hasty departure from his post after James II took flight from England in 1688.
Included in the list of titles are thirteen in English, forty-nine
in French, and two in Italian, covering historical and political
thought, drama, poetry, religion, and education, and including
works by Greek and Latin authors (in French translation). While
Etherege's own books may never be recovered, a full bibliography of
the titles and contents might prove useful to anyone wishing to find
out more about Etherege--his reading and his wide and varied inter-
ests.

Occasionally Etherege's close friends and contemporaries spoke in
letters or poetry of his idle habits: Dryden addressed him as "O
thou imortall source of Idleness," and Rochester accused him of "th'
crying sin [of] Idleness." But perhaps these remarks were speaking
of Etherege's pose, not of his real character. He did put together
three popular and lasting dramas; he did serve in two diplomatic
posts under two different kings; and he did carry on a regular and
extensive correspondence with a number of people--official and
unofficial--during his stay at Ratisbon. Even if biographical material is wanting, we are left with an impressive amount of written
material, about which can be said that much of it is prose of a very
high quality. Dryden, indeed, said as much when he called Etherege
"the undoubted best author of [prose] which our nation has produced."

Theatre History
Literary criticism, theatrical history, and biography make up
the bibliography of a poet and playwright. Since most of the work
on Etherege has been done by literary and dramatic critics, especially during the twentieth century, theatre history does not figure
largely in this bibliography. Yet I insist on considering the
theatricality of the plays; they are not closet dramas. The popularity of The Comical Revenge; or, Love in a Tub (1664) and The Man
of Mode; or, Sir Fopling Flutter (1676) was assured from their
opening performances, and this lasted well into the eighteenth century. Less auspicious was the opening of She Wou'd if She Cou'd
(1668), as Pepys recorded in his Diary of 6 February of that year
(1668.B1), but the play gained some favor and was occasionally
performed through the early eighteenth century. By the middle of
the century, however, there were almost no performances (one or two
in odd seasons), and Etherege's plays were dropped from the repertoires of the London companies and from those in the provinces. For
more than fifty years they remained in oblivion.

Despite the recommendations for revivals of Etherege's comedies
by Hazlitt (1819.B1) and Lamb (1822.B1), the plays were virtually
excluded from the nineteenth-century stage because of their alleged
immorality (see Olshen, 1972.B12). Changes in critical and theatrical attitudes in the twentieth century have assured Etherege a fairer

hearing. The comedies are now seen not only as historically important, but also as significant in their own right. Certainly Etherege the playwright has regained some stature in recent years, yet a
revival of one of the plays is somewhat of a rarity. The comedies
are, indeed, worthy of theatrical attention and deserve, like much
of Restoration drama, more perfomances; the plays provide good
entertainment and are at the same time amusing satires on the manners and the eccentricities of individuals.

Despite the infrequency of the staging of Etherege's plays, they
have appeared more in the past ten years than in the previous two
hundred. Two recent revivals cited are 1971.B11 and 1979.B5. While
the ambiguity of the resolutions of the plays pose some difficulties
for modern audiences, the playwright is applauded for his observations on human nature, for his insight in drawing character, and
for his ability to create comic situations. As the words move from
page to stage, the literay critic may be able to take another view
of the text. Much of the recent philosophically oriented criticism
(which does perhaps attempt to rescue Etherege from the condemnation of L. C. Knights--1937.B1) could inform good theatrical performances.

Etherege, it seems to me, has something to say to our age about
the individual and society, about people's hang-ups and foibles.
His light touch and verbal wit will not make changes in society or
revolutionize the times, but they can continue to delight theatre
audiences and readers alike.

Texts

(a) Editions of the Plays
    The first collected edition of the plays was printed at the
beginning of the eighteenth century (1704.A1) and reprinted for
several decades (1715.A1; 1723.A1; 1735.A1), before losing popularity. The first modern edition of the plays, based on the 1704 text,
was prepared by A. W. Verity (1888.A1). For several decades, interest in Etherege increased, and in 1927 (1927.A1), H. F. B. Brett-
Smith edited the plays and provided a lengthy introduction with
textual and critical notes, using the first quartos of the plays.
Still the standard text for Etherege's dramatic work, the Brett-
Smith edition provides a great amount of collateral information
about the man and his plays. Currently, Shirley Strum Kenny is at
work on a new edition of the plays for the Clarendon Press, Oxford.

(b) Poetry
    Brett-Smith has proposed an edition of the poems to follow The
Dramatic Works, but because of his untimely death this was never
completed. It remained for James Thorpe to publish a definitive
edition of the poems (1963.A1) with extensive notes and commentary.

(c) Letters
    The Letterbook of Etherege was published by Sybil Rosenfeld (1928.
A1), who in subsequent articles describes other collections of letters that came to light later (1934.B5 and 1952.B4). Frederick

Bracher edited and put together these several volumes of correspondence with other letters he discovered in <u>Letters of Sir George
Etherege</u> (1974.A1). It is occasionally necessary, however, to use
both editions because they do not print the same letters.
(d) Individual Works
    (1) <u>The Comical Revenge; or, Love in a Tub</u>
    There is no separate modern English edition of Etherege's first
play, yet in his own day, <u>Love in a Tub</u> (its popular title) was the
most reprinted of the plays (1667.A1; 1669.A1, A2; 1689.A1; 1690.A1;
and 1697.A1). A Russian translation was published in the last
decade (1975.A1).
    (2) <u>She Wou'd if She Cou'd</u>
    A modern spelling edition by Charlene M. Taylor in the Regents
Restoration Drama Series (1972.A1) provides a thorough introduction
and explanatory notes. There has been a Polish translation (1962.
A2), and a Russian text of the play has been proposed (1976.B10).
    (3) <u>The Man of Mode; or, Sir Fopling Flutter</u>
    The most popular of Etherege's plays, it has been frequently
anthologized in the twentieth century. Separate editions have been
prepared by W. B. Carnochan (1966.A1; modern spelling), John Conaghan
(1973.A1; old spelling), and John Barnard (1979.A1; old spelling
with some modernizing for clarity and consistency). Each of these
three editions includes detailed critical introductions and notes.
Barnard, it should be added, thoroughly reviews significant scholarship on the play. Some scenes have been translated into French
(1967.A1).
(e) Concordance
    David Mann is preparing a concordance to the plays and poetry for
Garland Press. The base texts are the Brett-Smith edition of the
plays (1927.A1) and the Thorpe edition of the poetry (1963.A1).

<u>General Critical Trends in Studies of Etherege</u>
    From relative obscurity, Etherege gained the attention of the
public with his first play, <u>The Comical Revenge; or, Love in a Tub</u>
(1664). This comedy combined heroic drama in verse with several
plots in prose--the love chase, gulling and duping, and a farce.
Such a combination proved extremely successful and brought Etherege
into acquaintance with several well-known courtiers, notably Lord
Buckhurst (with whom he exchanged bawdy verse epistles), the Earl
of Rochester, Sir Charles Sedley, and the Duke of Buckingham.

    His next play, <u>She Wou'd if She Cou'd</u> (1668), dropped the heroic
plot and concentrated more on character--developing a pair of witty
lovers, a would-be cuckold, his seemingly respectable wife, and a
drinking, wenching country knight. Lots of intrigue is mixed with a
little farce. Despite the under-rehearsed opening (see Pepys, 1668.
B1), the comedy was appreciated by two fellow playwrights--Thomas
Shadwell (1671.B2) and John Dennis (1702.B1)--and earned the ap-
proval of the Court.

    Etherege's third play, <u>The Man of Mode; or, Sir Fopling Flutter</u>

(1676), is, by contemporary and present-day standards, one of the cleverest comedies of manners ever written, and certainly a dramatic triumph of the age. It is one of the many ironies in Etherege's life that by the time he was an established playwright and one of the great comic dramatists of the day, he had discontinued writing plays. He had apparently demonstrated his ability to those courtiers who were his friends, and he did not care to write for fame, fortune, or posterity. In his offhanded way, Etherege published these plays, wrote poems from time to time, engaged in witty correspondence, but he did not seem greatly concerned with the production of these trifles. Perhaps his courtier friends were right: he was "gentle George," "easy Etherege."

Although traditional literary history claims that Etherege launched the "comedy of manners" with She Wou'd if She Cou'd, this view has recently been challenged by Robert D. Hume (1972.B7). While we know from one of Etherege's contemporaries, the playwright Thomas Shadwell, that the play was not a popular success, the fault of ill-prepared players, Shadwell still believed it "the best comedy that has been written since the Restauration of the Stage" (1671. B2). The contradiction between contemporary and current views brings out a real problem of critical evaluation and highlights theatrical evolution. If Etherege was not the founder of the "comedy of manners," he certainly set standards for contemporary playwrights. Furthermore, his plays remained popular, were often reprinted, and were frequently acted over the next sixty years.

After 1736, however, reprints of Etherege's plays were discontinued, they were seldom staged, and finally they dropped out of the repertoire all together, especially after The Man of Mode was cried down in the 1750s by a generation of theatregoers who had been raised on sentimental comedy. In the latter half of the eighteenth century, Etherege was only of slight interest to a few historians and antiquarians (and those not always accurate in their handling of facts). Mrs. Inchbald must have thought him too risqué to include in her collection of plays at the end of the century, showing that lip service to morality and Mrs. Grundy were abroad.

Lamb, in the London Magazine (1822.B1), and Hazlitt in his lectures at the Surr[e]y Institution (1819.B1), commented approvingly on Etherege, but Macaulay probably killed all interest with his scathing remarks on the Restoration dramatists which were included in Hunt's anthology of 1840 (1841.B1). Even though Hunt omitted Etherege, Macaulay pillories Sir George, along with those playwrights who were included--Congreve, Wycherley, Vanbrugh, and Farquhar.

For the next forty years, Etherege was seldom more than a brief entry in literary histories (a developing genre in the latter half of the nineteenth century), significant or notorious because he was a friend of that rake Rochester. Thus, much of the criticism in the two hundred years after the first performances of Etherege's plays dealt with the immorality of both the plays and the playwright. Many critics and literary historians tended to dismiss Etherege's comedies on the grounds that if they were vulgar, they could have no aesthetic value. Even though some critics admitted a certain stylistic elegance, the plays were generally considered licentious, and only fit to be read for historical reasons. Other interest centered on the people who were the real life models of Etherege's dramatic characters; Rochester, for example, was the prototype for Dorimant. Indeed, a French writer of the day (see 1857.B1) uses the smart dialogue of Dorimant to show how clever Rochester was in conversation.

In 1881, Edmund Gosse published an essay in Cornhill Magazine which changed the direction of studies of Sir George Etherege. Using the letters (1685-8) that had been in the British Museum since 1838 (even Macaulay had seen them), Gosse reexamined the playwright's character and plays. Etherege, Gosse found, was an important and innovative dramatist, a writer of graceful prose, and a good diplomat.

Gradually over the next thirty years, Etherege came into fashion as a playwright worthy of attention and even of serious study. An especially popular topic, mentioned by Gosse, was the influence of Molière on Restoration comedy generally, and on Etherege in particuar. What these studies show is that Etherege knew French, probably traveled in France, and perhaps even saw some of Molière's productions. Nevertheless, while Etherege may have been influenced by the Frenchman, his comedy is in the main English. The studies which claim that Etherege was influenced by Molière tend to be based more on opinion and conjecture than on solid facts.

Restoration playwrights were also the subject of German dissertations, such as 1901.A1. These studies tended to be on "the life and works" of a dramatist. Looking back on these productions from a modern perspective, one finds them detailed and inclusive, but unimaginative. They are, nevertheless, an important step in the history of the study of Restoration drama insofar as they do go into detail, present many facts, and take the plays seriously.

The study of Restoration comedy in the first eighty years of the twentieth century mirrors, in a way, the writing of it just after the Cromwellian interregnum. After any war, there is the possibility of a turning to a more open and freer way of seeing the world. These Restoration comedies, in which the morals of the last age carry little weight with the new generation, seem to grow in popularity at times when old ways and old-fashioned models are being rejected. Those who usually find Restoration comedy to their taste are frequently people who are willing to try out new ideas, who reject the status quo, and who are willing to drop prejudices and preconceptions. They are attracted to Restoration comedy by the verbal wit and the lack of sentimentality, by the tough truths and the absence of easy platitudes, and by the realistic answers and by the freedom from worn-out clichés.

Palmer (1913.B3) and Nettleton (1914.B1) set a new course in studies of Restoration comedy, or of the "comedy of manners," as Palmer calls these dramas. They appreciate the plays as plays and do not make a moral football of them. After the First World War, others took up the study of these neglected dramas, and in the 1920s interest in plays and playwrights of the Restoration bloomed. For the first time, full editions of the major playwrights were issued with notes and commentary: Congreve (edited by Montague Summers, 1923), Wycherley (edited by Summers, 1924), Congreve (edited by Dobrée, 1925-28), Etherege (edited by Brett-Smith, 1927), Shadwell (edited by Summers, 1927), Vanbrugh (edited by Webb and Dobrée, 1928), Sedley (edited by Pinto, 1928), Farquhar (edited by Stonehill, 1930), Congreve (edited by Bateson, 1930), and Otway (edited by Gosch, 1932). Criticism formed part of the reappraisal, and along with the work of other Restoration dramatists, Etherege's work is freshly examined by Krutch (1924.B3), Dobrée (1924.B2), Perry (1925.B4), and Lynch (1926.B3). Biographical detail is dug out by Foster (1922.B1, B2, B3, B4; 1927.B3; 1928.B3), and a brief, though somewhat inaccurate, life was written by Dobrée (1925.B1). Brett-Smith, in his introduction to The Dramatic Works (1927.A1), knits together what is known about Etherege's personal history and with her edition of the Letterbook (1928.A1), Sybil Rosenfeld opened Sir George's diplomatic years to wider study. The economic depression of the 1930s finds a corresponding dropping away of the studies of Restoration comedy. During this decade, too, L. C. Knights fulminated against the genre, charging that these plays were "trivial, gross, and dull" (1937.B1).

After the Second World War, there was again a renewed and expanded interest in Restoration comedy. Many books and articles came out of dissertations (for example, Mignon, 1947.B2; Smith, 1948.B3); other works are fruits of this continued interest in Restoration drama (Sherburn, 1948.B2; Wilson, 1948.B4). In the next decade, Underwood prepared the first modern full-length study of Etherege's plays (1952.A2; 1957.A1). During the same era, books and articles appear studying various aspects of, among other playwrights, Etherege: wit is studied by Fujimura (1952.B1), women by Gagen (1954.B2), the précieuse tradition by Berkeley (1955.B2, B3; 1959.B1), and appearance and reality by Holland (1959.B3). Knight's damning criticism of Restoration comedy (1937.B1) is addressed by Bateson (1957.B2) among other supporters of the genre.

In the early 1960s, the appearance of the first volumes of The London Stage, 1660-1800 provided a vast quantity of information to students of Restoration drama, challenging them to discover more about the facts surrounding the productions and the development of the theatrical milieu (see 1960.B1; subsequent volumes were printed in 1961.B4; 1962.B7; 1965.B9; and 1968.B8). A couple of critics,

Introduction

prior to the publication of The London Stage, did make some observations about the "early phase" of Restoration comedy--1934.B3 and
1951.B4. More recently this first decade has been studied with The
London Stage calendars and apparatus at hand. Hume (1972.B7), for
example, explores the diversity and development of the theatre from
1660 to 1679; Pirages (1977.B7) discusses the variety of experimentation; and Kavenik (1977.B5) focuses on the repertoire system of
the 1660s. Such uses of The London Stage volumes will give us a
more accurate picture of the acting companies and of popular trends;
it will also provide documentation to support conclusions arising
from research about the decades when Etherege was writing.

Judith Milhous, Robert Hume, and Arthur Scouten are now at work
on a revision of the first two volumes of The London Stage, from
1660 to 1717, which will include many more performance dates and
provide additional details about the theatrical world at the end of
the seventeenth century. Also, The Biographical Dictionary of Actors
and Actresses, 1660-1800, compiled by Philip Highfill, Kalmin
Burnham, and Edward Langhans (Southern Illinois University Press),
now in progress, should be used as a companion volume to The London
Stage. The Dictionary will provide researchers with an even greater
amount of detailed information about people in the theatrical world,
their roles, their careers, and their lives on and off of the stage.

The difficulty of categorizing the drama from 1660 to 1710 has
caused literary and theatre historians many problems. Clearly
Etherege's Love in a Tub of 1664 is not the same kind of comedy as
Farquhar's Constant Couple (1704), yet an early critic (1928.B9)
lumps all the comedies written during this forty-year period under
the category of "artificial comedy." Perhaps more viable sugges-
tions are made by Smith (1948.B3), who divides the comedies (excluding the sentimental) into three phases: "gay comedy," 1660-75;
"cynical comedy," 1675-87; and "exemplary comedy," 1687-1707.
Sherburn's division, made in the same year (1948.B2), separates the
comedies into "movements": 1668-76 and 1693-1707. Scouten (1966.
B19) argues for a similar division of 1668-76 and 1691-1707, whereas
Hume (1972.B7) considers that the early period of Restoration comedy
covers 1660-79. Whatever division is made, Etherege is certainly in
the vanguard; his first two plays are historically significant, and
popular, if not influential. His third play is a triumph of the
genre. Moreover, Etherege's comedies serve as models for the next
generation of comic dramatists, Congreve, Vanbrugh, Cibber, and
Farquhar, who alter his vision of Charles II's society to fit their
own society under William and Mary.

Topics of Criticism

Having dealt with the chronological development of the criticism
of Etherege, I feel that it would be useful to the researcher to
examine the topics that have been treated in the various interpreta-
tions of Etherege's work. By this means, one can, perhaps, gain a
different perspective on the patterns that make up Etherege's critical reputation.

Introduction

Much of the earlier commentary on Etherege's work was devoted to
its immorality. For this reason, as I have already noted, Etherege's
plays went into eclipse for almost two-hundred years. The following epithets which describe the comedies suggest why they were
seldom read and never performed: "extremely loose" (1753.B1); "dan-
gerous" (1800.B1); "lascivious" (1838.B1); "licentious" (1864.B2),
and "vulgar" (1876.B2). Frequently the plays are condemned, while
the language receives faint praise for its style or elegance. Contemporary with these remarks, a few minority voices still commend
the plays: "modesty of language" (1784.B1); "the best comedy we
have" (1798.B1); "an exquisite . . . picture . . . of that age"
(1819.B1); and "effective restraint in satire" (1893.B2). If Lamb
(1822.B1) enjoyed the plays because of their aesthetic appeal,
Knights (1937.B1) disliked them on the same grounds. And a later
critic, who set out to answer Knights, ended by agreeing with him
(1964.B9). Another critic remarks that Restoration comedies lack
any dramatic quality (1970.B6). Andrew Bear (1972.B2) reviews the
arguments of moral versus literary judgment and takes up Knights in
a thoroughgoing answer, dealing with the issues point by point.

Of the other critics who have undertaken a review of the criticism of Restoration comedy, drama, and stage, one (1922.B5) finds
Etherege the instigator of putting "these unmoral times" into the
theatre. Others, however, try to chart the critical ebb and flow
(1963.B5; 1966.B12; 1967.B7; 1978.B6).

Apart from general critical reviews, however, what subjects do
commentators find the most alluring in Etherege's plays? As he
wrote in an age of rakes and libertines, these two closely related
topics are frequently selected for study. Underwood (1957.A1) sees
two principal traditions of male protagonists: the honest man and
the libertine. These conflicting characters with opposite philosophical points of view create much of the tension in the comedies.
A different approach is taken by Wall (1963.B8), who compares the
protagonists with actual people in the Court, and who finds that the
rakes "are not realistic." Traugott (1966.B21) sees in the "rake's
progress" the rake-heroes's re-definition of love and honor, whereas
Jordan (1972.B9) examines two types of libertines: the extravagant
rake and the gentleman rake. These protagonists are also found to
have structural functions in the comedies (1973.B2), to suffer from
"comic shallowness" (1975.B3), or to have affinities with the
dandies of the late nineteenth century (1973.B13). Novak (1977.B6)
looks at the entire "libertine offensive" of the 1670s as a division
of the town and the country. The usual Restoration rake character,
with the exception of Dorimant, is put down by Hume (1977.B4) as
"seldom anything but [a] comic exaggeration." And while Dorimant
may be tough, he is "tamed by a woman even tougher."

Because of the importance of the clever, strong-minded women in

Etherege, it is not too surprising to find these heroines a subject
of many writers. Gagen (1954.B2) sees several of these heroines as
"women in command," Lightfoot (1973.B10) asserts that these women
have "more intellectual and social freedom than was available to
[most females] in England from 1660 to 1700," and McDonald (1976.B6)
finds that they are self-aware and self-determined. Moreover, there
is, according to Young (1977.B10) a "greater maturity" in the female
protagonists; he notes especially Ariana, Gatty, and Harriet.

Research has also included investigation of marriage laws (1942.
B2; 1977.B1), marriages of convenience (1962.B8), the importance of
money in marriage (1971.B2), the uses of marriage (1975.B2), and
marital discord (1977.B3). Marriage may carry with it a moral purpose (1954.B5), or it can be used for comic effects (1975.B10).
Although "love of power" (1974.B1) leads indirectly to marriage, it
must ultimately give way to the power of love (1962.B3).

Besides the studies on the action and interaction of the principal characters, there are related writings on a number of "type
characters" that show up in Restoration comedy, including the plays
of Etherege. Along with the gay couple (1948.B3), come older people
(1947.B1), the family (1960.B2), friends (1956.B2), servants (1960.
B4), cuckolds (1962.B5), fops (1965.B3), and social climbers (1965.
B8).

Many people have written on Etherege's sources (or lack of them--
1691.B1), for example, in Molière and the précieuse tradition. These
French influences have been studied by scholars on both sides of the
Channel and on both sides of the Atlantic. Gosse's article (1881.
B2) and subsequent book (1883.B1), which mentions Molière as a possible source, is responsible for many of the early twentieth-century
studies--1906.B2, B3; 1907.B1; 1910.B1; and 1913.B1. Wilcox's dis-
sertation (1931.B3), and his later book (1938.B2), disposes of many
of these earlier views. But the subject has not yet been closed as
can be seen from three post-Second World War studies--1946.B3; 1949.
B3; and 1961.B1. As recently as 1980.B1, Bracher reminds us of
Etherege's debt to Molière in The Man of Mode: "If Etherege were in
Paris in 1659, he could have seen the first production there of
Molière's Les Précieuses Ridicules at the theatre du Petit-Bourbon.
From this play Etherege borrowed heavily in The Man of Mode: the
fop from Paris, his explanation of his song, the catalogue of clothes
and perfume, and the footmen named after the provinces, Champagne,
Picard, Bourgignon." The précieuse elements were first studied in
detail by Lynch (1926.B3), but the later critics Berkeley (1955.B2
and 1959.B1) and Cecil (1959.B2) have pushed the topic further in
order to help us understand many of the compromises made in the
plays.

Another tradition that has been followed in Etherege's plays is
the Jonsonian humours. Following a study by Clancy (1947.B1),
Lewis (1973.B9) sees that there is a combined tradition of humours

that binds the comedies together. On the other hand, Riddell (1966. B18) feels that Etherege "seemed to care very little about [humours characters]." But the real backgrounds of Etherege's plays are not in Jonson, but in Middleton's comedies, according to Bruce (1974. B1). Weiss (1953.B3), taking another tack, believes that the plays are less indebted to a literary genealogy, but more dependent on Hobbesian philosophy.

The Restoration period, especially Restoration drama, can be said to be the source of a theme that develops and becomes strong in the eighteenth century--the sentimental. A number of studies are devoted to this literary subject that carried over into the life of the later age. Early scholars writing on sentimentalism tend to find little of it in Etherege's plays, yet Croissant (1935.B1) does detect elements of sentimentality in both Love in a Tub and The Man of Mode. Germer (1963.B2) agrees that sentiment does occur in "the love and honor" plot of the former play. But many critics find Etherege too tough-minded to admit this "debased romanticism."

Whether or not satire precludes sentiment has been a matter of frequent concern to critics. If satire does preclude sentiment, is or is not Etherege a satirist? McDonald (1964.B7) believes he is because the plays avoid preconceptions: Etherege, thus, writes "complexly and conciously moral comedies." On the other side of the argument, Hymas (1964.B4) finds that Etherege rejects the satiric attitude in favor of the comic. Jantz (1978.B4) finds satiric "targets" in the plays, whereas Dietz (1972.B5), studying the plot structure, determines that the plays are organized by irony and satire, and are, consequently, different from comedies at the end of the century. Hume (1973.B5) believes that there is no neat, tidy theory that will apply to all comedy of the period, and noting the contrasts of "example" on the one hand and of "ridicule" on the other, wishes to make readers skeptical "of all inclusive statements about this drama."

Obscure references in the texts of Etherege's plays have been examined in 1824.B1 (Love in a Tub); 1888.B2 (The Man of Mode); 1929.B1 (Love in a Tub); 1961.B1 (The Man of Mode); and 1968.B5 (The Man of Mode); and an annotation proposed in 1978.B3 (She Wou'd if She Cou'd). Some of Etherege's lines have analogues in works by Donne (1958.B3), Cowley (1927.B4), and less well known poets (1945. B3). Dorimant's quotations from many of Waller's poems cause Berman (1970.B1) to investigate the structural implications of this usage: ultimately, he finds that the repetition of Waller's verses is dropped by Dorimant because the heroic ideals no longer apply to the new romance with Harriet.

Etherege's own poetry appears to be in the courtly tradition of verses, thrown off to amuse and surprise his friends. In some instances, distinguishing his poetry from that of other Restoration poets is difficult. Before Thorpe's edition of the poetry of

Introduction

Etherege (1963.A1), much of previous scholarship had been concerned
with attribution (1939.B1; 1959.B5), classification (1944.B1; 1963.
B4), and the placing of Etherege in relation to other courtier poets
of the Restoration (1954.B4). Since Thorpe's text has come out,
Pinto (1965.B4) has evaluated the court poets; he praises Etherege's
ability to use other voices than that of a court gallant, finding his
verse an "attractive mixture of innocence and sophistication."
Miner (1974.B6) discusses Etherege's contribution to various poetical conventions, and concludes that Etherege's character is a
"puzzle." It is, perhaps, this very enigma which draws some people
back to a study of the plays and the poetry in hopes of finding
"the figure in the carpet" of Etherege's language.

<u>Individual Works</u>
   Much of the criticism in this section has been cited in preceding
sections, but the intention in focusing on the three plays is to
assist a researcher to grasp the trends of the critical patterns as
they emerge in each play.

<u>The Comical Revenge; or, Love in a Tub</u>
   The charge that <u>Love in a Tub</u> is Etherege's weakest play can be
answered in at least three ways: 1) it was the first play of a
novice playwright, 2) it was followed by two plays that were even
better, or 3) even though it combined a number of popular forms of
the day, it is innovative in its use of language and in its drawing
of character. Downes, the prompter at the Duke's playhouse, where
all of Etherege's plays had their premières, mentions the great
success of <u>Love in a Tub</u> in his early history of Restoration plays
(1708.B1); it brought in a thousand pounds the first season. Ward
(1899.B2) attributes the play's success to its realism in the prose
scenes. Krutch (1924.B3), on the other hand, considers it old
fashioned: "it might have been written before the civil war."
Nevertheless, the Widow Rich-Sir Frederick plot is cited by Kronenberger (1952.B3) as original to Etherege, not something adapted from
Caroline drama. The rhymed sections of the love and honor plot,
however, have caused some readers trouble (1779.B1; 1952.B2); yet one
critic sees wit in the comedy as equal to honor in tragedy, using
<u>Love in a Tub</u> as his primary example (1967.B4). The language, of
course, divides the "low" plots in prose from the "high" plot in
verse. This contrast of the language is explored by Berkeley (1955.
B3).

   Recent criticism has tended to discover a unity in the four plots
of <u>Love in a Tub</u>. Kishi (1972.B10), for example, sees that the
plots are all variations on one idea--"honourable heroic actions."
And what may look like disunity is, in fact, an ambivalent attitude
on the part of the playwright. Scouten (1976.B9) finds unity in the
play's episode and imagery. Hume (1972.B7; 1976.B3) surveys the
theatrical scene and finds that all four plots were popular <u>before</u>
Etherege and that Etherege's most skillful contribution was the
ability to blend together heroic elements, gulling, humourous court-
ship, and farce.

xxvii

Introduction

She Wou'd if She Cou'd

A number of approaches have been taken in appraising Etherege's second comedy. Bell (1866.B1) pointed out the various intrigues, and these are also mentioned by Krutch (1924.B3). Another way of perceiving the action of the comedy is Dobrée's description (1924. B2) of She Wou'd if She Cou'd as a ballet. Ward (1899.B2) comments on the brilliant dialogue; whereas the importance of language (and character) for Hume (1972.B7) is that it evolves from the plot. The action steers a course between wit and virtue for Daiches (1960.B3), whereas Barber (1957.B1) sees a tension created in honor and would-be honor, especially in the character of Lady Cockwood. Montgomery (1929.B3) sees the young women, Ariana and Gatty, becoming honest, while at the same time Lady Cockwood, who prizes her "reputation for virtue . . . more highly . . . than virtue itself," remains static despite her attempts at extra-marital sexual intrigue. The conflicts of the city and the country are discussed by Tatum (1960. B5), Barnard (1971.B1), and Novak (1977.B6), who, while he does not discuss She Wou'd if She Cou'd, provides a good background of the antagonism emerging in the late sixties. For Scouten (1969.B9), the play is the triumph of experience over hope.

Charlene M. Taylor, in her introduction to the Regents Restoration edition (1972.A1), argues that Etherege's second comedy fuses social, romantic, artificial, and intellectual strains. Since She Wou'd if She Cou'd is the first Restoration comedy to combine these elements, it should be considered the first comedy of manners. In the same year, Hume (1972.B7) took an opposite position: the play did not launch the comedy of manners; Etherege was not an initiator of a new mode, and neither did She Wou'd if She Cou'd have a significant influence on the comedy that followed. Almost fifty years earlier, Lynch (1926.B3) had confidently proclaimed that in She Wou'd if She Cou'd "the main course of the development of Restoration comedy had been determined." Nevertheless, the questionable popularity of the play with audiences, including the first one (1668.B1), makes it necessary to examine She Wou'd if She Cou'd in the light of more recent discoveries. Perhaps it is just this evolutionary question, "what is the first comedy of manners?", that may help us arrive at a greater understanding of the play itself, and of the Restoration comic tradition. As Taylor and Hume demonstrate, we can either consider themes within the plays that are picked up by later playwrights or examine audience reaction and subsequent revivals of the play in the period. Hume, in his Development of the English Drama in the late Seventeenth Century (1976.B3), does, in fact, look at both theatre history and at themes. He considers Etherege's social focus too narrow and feels that the emphasis in She Wou'd if She Cou'd is on character, not on action. His conclusion that "Etherege is not a norm for his time," is balanced by his consideration that the play is "unique." By this term, I take it, he means that She Wou'd if She Cou'd achieves something that other plays at the end

of the decade do not. This elusive, special quality, then, may have
created for other playwrights a level of achievement to which they
wished to aspire. Possibly it is a playwright's play. While it
was not slavishly copied, it still might have become for the next
decade a standard of achievement to be surpassed.

The Man of Mode; or, Sir Fopling Flutter

The Man of Mode has been acclaimed by supporters and by detrac-
tors of Restoration comedy as demonstrably Etherege's best work. It
has brought forth a great deal of critical commentary, some of it
quite contradictory. Early audiences were intrigued by the possible
real life prototypes of Dorimant (was it Rochester?), Sir Fopling
(Beau Hewytt or Sir Car Scroope?), and of other characters in the
cast. Osborn, in his edition of Spence's Anecdotes (1966.B20), collects contemporary views and later opinions. Recently Sherbo (1949.
B4) and Hammond (1973.B4) eliminated the possibility that Beau Hewytt
was Sir Fopling; but Auffret (1966.B1) suggests Moll Kirke as a
candidate for Mrs. Loveit, and Charles Mordaunt for Sir Fopling.
Vieth (1959.B5) finds parallels of The Man of Mode in Rochester's
work. But all this identification of possible models for the characters has obscured serious critical study of the play itself. Mainly, it has been twentieth-century critics who have restored The Man
of Mode to the mainstream of Restoration comedy.

Yet even in this century, the play has been variously labeled:
"ruthless" (1970.B6), "without compassion" (1961.B2), "vituperative"
(1960.B6), "too cruel" (1942.B2), and "cynical" (1929.B4). Davies
(1969.B2), who calls the play "uncompromisingly tough and realistic,"
has summed up many critical opinions about the play in this phrase.
Other recent critics find the play "not necessarily profound" (1972.
B7) and feel that gamesmanship is the order of the play (1970.B2;
1972.B6). Still others explore "the comic punishment" (1977.B2) and
the "rebellious liberation" of Dorimant (1969.B6). Wit in The Man of
Mode has been studied in detail by Feltham (1951.B3) and Fujimara
(1952.B1); the comic spirit by Perry (1925.B4) and Birdsall (1970.
B2); tone and style by Hartman (1974.B5); the social elements by
Lynch (1926.B3) and Hawkins (1972.B6); the comedy of experience by
Powell (1965.B5); and the experimental qualities by Rodway (1972.
B13).

One question to be resolved right away by the readers or the
audience is asked by Barnard (1971.B1; 1979.A1) and Hume (1972.B8):
How is the audience to take Dorimant? Barnard, who raises this
question, also adds these qualifications: "the audience . . . cannot
merely watch, but must judge and choose between the characters and
their deeds . . . within the standards set up by the play's domi-
nant concepts." Audience reaction depends partly on their degree of
involvement or detachment with Dorimant and the rest of the cast.
In the human relationships played out on stage, Dorimant moves from
the dispassionate letter he is sending Mrs. Loveit, when the play
opens, to an overzealous involvement with Harriet, which makes him

"renounce all the joys I have in friendship and wine, sacrifice to you all the interest I have in other women . . . ." If we have identified with Dorimant, we are brought up sharply when, just prior to his declaration to Harriet, he finds he has overextended himself and becomes embroiled with both Loveit and Belinda: "I was never at such a loss before." For some in the audience, The Man of Mode provides a tale of the deceiver deceived, and they delight in seeing Dorimant meet his match in Harriet. For others, the ambiguity of Dorimant's character, and most of the characters on stage do not know how to take his actions, makes identification with him difficult. If one finds no sympathetic character, the detachment can cause a loss of interest in the play. What keeps one's attention may be the delicate equilibrium Etherege manages to maintain on stage between involvement and detachment, desire and prudence, passion and self-control, surrender and freedom.

The audience must also resolve the conflict between the private individual and the public self. In the play, characters must take chances; while in most of the risk-taking they could gain for themselves new social freedoms, they could also suffer personal loss-- of respectability, of poise, of control. Even in the last scene where there is a reestablishment of some norms, the conclusion does not resolve all actions of the play to the satisfaction of the audience. Dorimant and Harriet, as well as the receptive playgoer, recognize the precariousness of their relationship. As Barnard (1979. A1) demonstrates, "The Man of Mode is not an entirely comforting or comfortable play. Its affirmation is balanced by an ironic skepticism."

Other extremes in the play that must be balanced by the audience are impulse and calculation (1969.B4), "covert and overt" emotions (1975.B4). Loftis (1972.B11), in fact, considers that it reveals "an emotional dimension of a sociological fact": although the play only pretends to be Restoration high life, it causes the audience to find a humanity about the characters that is missing from the recent statistical studies made about the age.

The rapport between the audience and the characters, a number of critics feel, is owing to Etherege's language. Harris (1965.B1), for example, shows how "similitudes from natural life offer a relationship to the human." For others, language distinguishes the true wit from the would-be wit (1952.B1; 1955.B1; 1965.B10; 1971.B6), and fops, fools, and grotesques have a language of their own (1965.B6; 1966.B5; 1976.B8). The conversations of the older people--Lady Woodvil and Old Bellair--show their ideas of social rank to be valueless (1947.B2; 1976.B1). Understanding the tone of heroic drama helps Martin (1976.B5) see Mrs. Loveit's language as supporting a hypocritical past and, thus, becoming a parody of heroic ideals.

Dorimant has been the most frequently studied character in the play. His relationship with Harriet gets a careful treatment from

Corman (1977.B2). In a different approach, Krause (1969.B6) finds the center of their relationship in "comic disobedience." Hume (1977.B4) sees Dorimant not as the typical exaggerated rake but as a tough-minded seducer of society belles, who is "tamed by a woman even tougher and more self-controlled than he." Being thus checked in his career, Dorimant is beaten at his own game, according to Simon (1963.B5).

Sir Fopling has been seen as a kind of would-be Dorimant, the form without the substance. Both can be considered men of mode (1969.B4). Scouten (1976.B9), for example, comments on the self-centeredness of both. If the audience is willing to tolerate one, then they will put up with the other: "the audiences natural indulgence for fools has a surprising relationship with its natural indulgence for rakes" (1979.A1). Thus, Sir Fopling is a comic counterpart of Dorimant (1971.B1), and helps define the rake-protagonist (1973.A1). Nevertheless, one critic points out that Dorimant and Medley pretend to accept Sir Fopling only to ridicule and entrap him (1969.B8). Critics also mention Sir Fopling's "monumental affectation" (1957.B2) and his narcissism (1962.B6), but the same epithets could also apply to Dorimant. Sutherland (1969.B10) believes that it is Sir Fopling who keeps the play from becoming a "dark comedy."

The conclusion of the play has seemed to many unresolved. Some critics express a concern that Harriet will discover that she has made a bad bargain and will regret her choice of a would-be reformed rake (1970.B9). Others believe that her "maturity" (1977.B10) and "judgment" (1976.B6) will enable her to overcome the obstacles still apparent at the end of the play. At the close of the play, problems arise from "crude verbal wit" (1965.B8), and what remains is still "ambivalent" (1969.B4). This leads to several critical attitudes toward the play: one critic finds no standard of values (1975.B9), another reckons it is not profound (1972.B7), and a third determines that even at his best Etherege's vision is only peripheral (1957.B3). Although the play may be only a "divertissement" (1972.B13), the unresolved conclusion makes the audience uneasy: the order of comedy gives way to the disorder of things as they are (1966.A1). Dorimant may have been educated "in the way of decorum" (1957.B2; 1966.B7) and his duality exposed (1962.B4; 1966.B10), but this is no cause for a celebration. In that Dorimant gets outsmarted, there may be some sense of rough poetical justice, but a decisive resolution there is not. Perhaps this is one of the points that Etherege is making: human interaction in the world continues because people just do not live happily ever after. He cannot honestly flatter our illusions, and leaves the play with its uncertain finish. Vieth (1977.B9) has noted the "relativity" in the Restoration consciousness, and it is nowhere better displayed than at the end of The Man of Mode. The relative place of an individual to others, then, not only creates shifting tensions throughout the play but also leaves the audience with a more complex attitude toward the difficulty in

real human relationships. Etherege's theatrical representation has
forced the audience to consider the social milieu and the place of
each individual in the relatively changing patterns of human life.

Conclusion
    Etherege has been the subject of an increasing amount of discus-
sion in books, articles, and dissertations; his plays are slowly
finding their way into the modern repertoire; and his role as a
diplomat is undergoing reappraisal. To class him with earlier dramatists, Shakespeare or Jonson, does him a disservice. He is not of
their stature. In the Restoration, only Dryden came near either of
them in quality or quantity. But given Etherege's small output and
the constraints of his time, he is a playwright who deserves to be
studied in relation to his fellow dramatists in the age of Charles
II. If the study of the text is balanced with more performances,
reader and audience alike can gain a historical perspective and a
view of human relations in a society that is challenging and enjoy-
able.

Acknowledgments
    I wish to acknowledge assistance from the following people:
Dr. William Wortman and Mrs. Sarah Barr (King Library, Miami Uni-
versity); Mrs. Patricia Hardesty (Oxford, Ohio); Professor Laurence
Bartlett (Ohio University); Professor Frederick Bracher (Santa
Barbara, California); Professor Robert D. Hume (Pennsylvania State
University); Professor Arthur Huseboe (Augustana College, Sioux Falls,
S. Dak.); Mr. Bernard Dhuicq (University of Paris, III); Professor
Pierre Danchin (University of Nancy, II), Professor Patricia
Tatspaugh (Prince Georges Community College, Largo, Md.); Professor
Albert Wertheim (Indiana University-Bloomington); and Ms. Judith
Hill (London, England). I should also like to express my apprecia-
tion to the staff of the Bodelian Library, Oxford, England; and the
staff of the North Library Reading Room of the British Library,
London, England. All these people went out of their way to help me
gain access to materials, to comment on preliminary checklists, to
provide copies of articles, or to assist in other ways. I would
also like to thank my editors, Janice Meagher and Professor Arthur
J. Weitzman for their help.

Writings by and about Etherege

<u>1664</u>

A BOOKS

1 ETHEREGE, GEORGE. <u>The Comical Revenge; or, Love in a Tub</u>.
   London: Henry Herringman, 92 pp.
      Wing E3367; W&M 543. Entered in The Stationers' Register
   8 July 1664.

2 _____. <u>The Comical Revenge; or, Love in a Tub</u>. London: Henry
   Herringman, 71 pp.
      Wing E3368; W&M 544.

B SHORTER WRITINGS

1 EVELYN, JOHN. The Diary, 27 April.
      Having seen the play on this date, Evelyn remarks that it
   is "a facetious comedy." See 1818.B1; 1879.B1; 1955.B5.

2 THE NEWES. 3 November, verso.
      Contains advertisement announcing the publication of <u>The
   Comical Revenge; or, Love in a Tub</u>, printed for Henry
   Herringman.

<u>1665</u>

A BOOKS--NONE

B SHORTER WRITINGS

1 PEPYS, SAMUEL. <u>The Diary</u>, 4 January.
      Calls <u>Love in a Tub</u> "very merry, but only so by gesture,
   no wit at all, which methinks beneath the [Duke's play] House."
   See 1825.B1; 1893.B1. 1968.B15.

<u>1666</u>

A BOOKS--NONE

1666

B SHORTER WRITINGS

1 PEPYS, SAMUEL. The Diary, 29 October.
        Calls Love in a Tub "a silly play." See 1825.B1; 1893.B1;
    1968.B15.

1667

A BOOKS

1 ETHEREGE, GEORGE. The Comical Revenge; or, Love in a Tub.
    London: Henry Herringman, 71 pp.
        Wing E3369; W&M 545. Reprint of 1664.A2.

B SHORTER WRITINGS--NONE

1668

A BOOKS

1 ETHEREGE, GEORGE. She Wou'd if She Cou'd. London: Henry
    Herringman, 92 pp.
        Wing E3378; W&M 555. Entered in The Stationers' Register,
    24 June 1668.

B SHORTER WRITINGS

1 PEPYS, SAMUEL. The Diary, 6 February.
        An eyewitness account of the first performance of She Wou'd
    if She Cou'd: "How full was the house and how silly the play,
    there being nothing in the world good in it." After the play,
    Pepys overheard Etherege "mightily find fault with the actors,
    that they were out of humour, and had not their parts perfect."
    On the last point, see 1671.B2. For diary references, see
    1825.B1; 1893.B1; 1968.B15.

2 _____. The Diary, 29 April.
        Sees Love in a Tub for a third time at the Duke of York's
    Playhouse. See 1825.B1; 1893.B1; 1968.B15.

1669

A BOOKS

1 ETHEREGE, GEORGE. The Comical Revenge; or, Love in a Tub.
    London: Henry Herringman, 71 pp.
        Wing E3370; W&M 546. Set, with catchword "the" on Sig.
    A_2r.

2

2 _____. The Comical Revenge; or, Love in a Tub. London: Henry
Harringman, 71 pp.
    Wing E3370a; W&M 547. Reset, with catchword "hope" on
Sig. A$_2$r.

B SHORTER WRITINGS

1 PEPYS, SAMUEL. The Diary, 1 February.
    Sees She Wou'd if She Cou'd for a second time, without
comment on its quality. See 1825.B1; 1893.B1; 1968.B15.

1671

A BOOKS

1 ETHEREGE, GEORGE. She Wou'd if She Cou'd. [London] In the Savoy:
Printed by T. N. for H. Herringman, 84 pp.
    Wing E3379; W&M 556. Reset from 1668.B1.

B SHORTER WRITINGS

1 KIRKMAN, FRANCIS. A True, Perfect, and exact Catalogue of all
Comedies, Tragedies, . . . etc., that were ever printed . . .
till . . . 1671. London: Francis Kirkman.
    Wing K637. Includes Love in a Tub and She Wou'd if She
Cou'd as comedies by George Etherege.

2 SHADWELL, THOMAS. The Humorists. London: H. Herringman, Sig.
[A$_4$].
    Wing S2851. In his "Preface," Shadwell comments that his
play was almost spoiled in its production because the actors
did not act it well. This imperfect action, he continues, is
"like to have destroy'd She would if she could, which I think
(and I have the Authority of some of the best Judges in
England for't) is the best comedy that has been written since
the Restauration of the Stage: And even that, for the imperfect representation of it at first, received such prejudice,
that, had it not been for the favour of the Court, in all
probability it had never got up again; and it suffers for it,
in a great measure to this very day." Reprinted in 1927.B5.

1675

A BOOKS--NONE

B SHORTER WRITINGS

1 PHILLIPS, EDWARD. Theatrum Poetarum. 2 vols. London: Charles

1676

Smith, Vol. 1, 192 pp., Vol. 2, 261 pp. 2:53.
Wing P2075. "George Etheridge a Comical writer of the
present Age; whose Two Comedies, Love in a Tub, and She would
if She could, for pleasant Wit, and no bad Oeconomy, are
judg'd not uuworthy [sic] the Applause they have met with."

1676

A BOOKS

1 ETHEREGE, GEORGE. The Man of Mode; or, Sir Fopling Flutter.
London: Printed by J. Macock, for Henry Herringman, 95 pp.
Wing E3374; W&M 551. Entered in The Stationers' Register,
15 June 1676.

*2 _____. "A Song in Sir Fopling Flutter." [London]: engrav'd by
Tho: Cross, n. d.
Wing E3380A; only known copy at W. A. Clark Library.
Thorpe (1963.A1, p. 145 suggests that the song dates from a
revival of The Man of Mode about 1698 for which Eccles (born
1668) composed the music. The poem, "Caelia with mournful
pleasure hears," Thorpe concludes, is not by Etherege.

B SHORTER WRITINGS

1 London Gazette. No. 1109. 3-6 July, verso.
An advertisement announcing the publication of The Man of
Mode, sold by Henry Herringman.

2 [MARVELL, ANDREW] Mr. Smirke; or, the Divine in Mode. London:
n. p.
Wing M873. Under the name of Andreas Rivetus, Jr., Marvell
attacked Francis Turner of Cambridge, author of Animadversions
on . . . The Naked Truth. Marvell's parody is based on Smirke,
a parson, who plays a brief role in The Man of Mode, V. ii.
See 1927.A1, p. xxvi; 1968.B12.

1680

A BOOKS--NONE

B SHORTER WRITINGS

1 [LANGBAINE, GERARD.] An Exact Catalogue of [Plays] . . . Printed
. . . till . . . 1680. Oxford: Printed by L. Lichfield for
Nicholas Cox.
Wing L373A. The compiler, apparently Langbaine (see 1688.
B1, B2), using earlier materials of Kirkman (1671.B1), cites

4

all three of Etherege's plays. See also remarks by D. S.
Rodes in his introduction to 1971.B3, a reprint of 1688.B1.

2 ROCHESTER, JOHN WILMOT, EARL OF. <u>Poems on Several Occasions</u>.
Antwerpen [probably London]: n.p.
    Wing R1753; Anr. State R1754. Etherege is mentioned in
several of the poems:
(1) "Satyr," p. 100. Probably written 1674.
    E[therege] writes <u>Airy Songs</u>, and <u>Soft Lampoons</u>,
    The best of any <u>Man</u>; as for your <u>Nouns</u>,
    <u>Grammar</u>, and <u>Rules of Art</u>, he knows 'em not,
    Yet writ two Talking <u>Plays</u> without one Plot.
    D. M. Vieth dates this poem, he has entitled "Timon," April-
June 1674 in his edition of Rochester, <u>Complete Poems</u> (New
Haven: Yale University Press, 1968), pp. 65-72.
(2) "A Session of the Poets," p. 103. Probably written 1675
or 1676.
    This Reverend Author [Dryden] was no sooner set by,
    But <u>Apollo</u> had got gentle George in his Eye,
    And frankly confest, of all Men that writ,
    There's none had more Fancy, Sence, Judgment and Wit.
    But i'th'crying Sin Idleness he was so hardn'd,
    That his long, Seven Years silence was not to be
      pardon'd.
    Evidence for attribution to Rochester can be found in George
de F. Lord's introduction to the poem in <u>Poems on Affairs of
State</u>, Vol. 1 (New Haven: Yale University Press, 1963), p.
352 [1963.B3]; or J. H. Wilson, <u>Review of English Studies</u>, 22
(1946), pp. 109-116, though Vieth in <u>Attribution in Restoration Poetry</u> (New Haven: Yale University Press, 1963) finds
the evidence of authorship indeterminate. Although Professor
Wilson suggests November or December 1676, this date does not
take into account the "seven years silence." Etherege had not
produced a play from 1668, but <u>The Man of Mode</u> had its premier
in the spring of 1676.
(3) "Imitation of Horace's 10th Satyr of the 1st Book," p. 40.
Probably written late 1675 or early 1676.
    <u>Shakespear</u> and <u>Johnson</u> did herein excell,
    And might herein be imitated well:
    Whom refin'd E[therege] copies not at all,
    But is himself a meer Original.
(4) "On Poet Ninny," p. 128. Probably written 1678.
    But never <u>satyr</u> did so softly bite,
    Or gentle George himself more gently write.

1682

A BOOKS--NONE

B SHORTER WRITINGS

1 DRYDEN, JOHN. "MacFlecknoe." London: D. Green.
Wing D2303. Probably written in the late 1670s (see
below). In the following lines, Dryden contrasts Etherege
with Flecknoe's heir, Shadwell. Lines 151-54; 183-84.
Let gentle George in triumph tread the stage,
Make Dorimant betray, and Loveit rage;
Let Cully, Cockwood, Fopling charm the pit,
And in their folly show the writer's wit.

When did his Muse from Fletcher scenes purloin,
As thou whole Eth'ridg dost transform to thine?

For the most recent discussion of dating see Vieth, 1979.
B7. Also consult the California Edition of Dryden, Works (Los
Angeles: University of California Press, 1972), 2:54-60
(poem); 2:301 (dating); 2:326 (Shadwell's borrowing from
Etherege). Or, Dryden, Works, ed. J. Kinsley (Oxford:
Clarendon Press, 1958), 4 vols., 1:265-71 (poem); 4-1913-22
(commentary).

2 RADCLIFFE, ALEXANDER. "News from Hell." In The Ramble. London:
Printed for the Author, and Sold by Walter Davis, p. 5.
Wing R529. Chides Etherege for thinking "a plot's too
gross for any play," and accuses the playwright of stealing
his dialogue from tavern conversation.

1683

A BOOKS--NONE

B SHORTER WRITINGS

1 [WOOD, THOMAS.] Juvenalis Redivivus. [London]: n.p., Printed
in the year 1683, pp. 17-18.
Wing W3410. A satire against poetasters, including
Etherege, in which Wood remarks on Etherege's gambling and his
recent marriage.

1684

A BOOKS

1 ETHEREGE, GEORGE. The Man of Mode; or, Sir Fopling Flutter.
London: Printed by J. Macock for H. Herringman, Sold by
J. Knight and F. Saunders. 81 pp.
Wing E3375; W&M cite two issues--552, with the headtitle
on [A4] in italics; 553, with the headtitle on [A4] in Roman
type.

B SHORTER WRITINGS

1 ETHEREGE, GEORGE. "See how fair Corinna lies." Song in Thomas
Southerne, The Disappointment, or The Mother in Fashion.
London: J. Hindmarsh, pp. 60-61.
Wing S4755. Lyrics and Music from V. S. ii. Reprinted
in Songs from Restoration Theater, ed. W. Thorpe (Princeton:
Princeton University Press, 1934), pp. 41-3; 1934.B9.

1685

A BOOKS--NONE

B SHORTER WRITINGS

1 ETHEREGE, GEORGE. "Tell me no more I am deceiv'd." Song in
Naham Tate, A Duke and No Duke. London: H. Bonwicke; pp.
45-47.
Wing T181. Lyric by Etherege, "set to music by Signoir
Baptist [Draghi?]." No indication where the song appeared
in the play. Lyrics and music reprinted in 1934.B9.

1687

A BOOKS--NONE

B SHORTER WRITINGS

1 WINSTANLEY, WILLIAM. Lives of the Most Famous English Poets.
London: H. Clark for Samuel Manship. p. 215.
Wing W3065. "Sir GEORGE ETHERIDGE, The Author of Two
Comedies, viz. Love in a Tub; and She Would if she Could;
which for pleasant Wit, and no bad Oeconomy, are judged not
unworrhy [sic] the applause they have met with." This cita-
tion follows Phillips (1675.B1) almost exactly; it omits The
Man of Mode.

1688

A BOOKS

1 ETHEREGE, GEORGE. An Account of the Rejoycing at the Dyet at
   Ratisbonne, Performed by Sir George Etherege, Kt., Residing
   there from His Majesty of Great Britain, upon Occasion of the
   Birth of The Prince of WALES: In a Letter to Himself.
   [London] In the Savoy: Edw. Jones, broadside.
       Wing E3366. Describes the celebration in Ratisbon of the
   birth of James II's son. Some party: it lasted for three
   days. See Bracher, Letters (1974.A1), pp. 279-85.

B SHORTER WRITINGS

1 LANGBAINE, GERARD. Momus Triumphans: or the Plagiaries of the
   English Stage . . . London: N[icholas] C[ox], sold by Sam.
   Holford, 1688 [1687].
       Wing L377. (Second issue with canceled titlepage bears
   the imprint "Printed for Nicholas Cox, and to be sold by him
   in Oxford, 1688 [1687]"; Wing L377A.) Using previously
   printed material (1671.B1 and 1680.B1), Langbaine here lists
   plays by author rather than by title as previous catalogues
   had done. Langbaine also footnotes all the borrowings
   ("plagiaries") he recognizes. It is significant that all of
   Etherege's plays are considered original and without analogue.
   See D. S. Rode's introduction to ARS reprint (1971.B3).

2 _____. A New Catalogue of English Plays, . . . London: for
   Nicholas Cox, and to be sold by him in Oxford, 1688, though a
   handwritten note in Bodley Wood E. 28(4), presumably by
   Anthony a Wood, says "published in the beginning of Dec.
   1687."
       Wing L377B. Embarrased by the "heathenish" title Momus
   Triumphans, Langbaine has a new title page (second cancel),
   a disclaimer ("Advertisement"), and an errata page (for the
   preface). Nevertheless, the rest of the catalogue remains
   the same from Sig. A2 on, except for a press variant on p. 7.
   See D. S. Rodes' introduction to ARS reprint (1971.B3), and
   1688.B1.

1689

A BOOKS

1 ETHEREGE, GEORGE. The Comical Revenge; or, Love in a Tub.
   London: H. Herringman, Sold by Francis Saunders. 71 pp.
       Wing E3371; W&M 548.

B SHORTER WRITINGS

1 GOULD, ROBERT. <u>Poems</u>. London: n.p., p. 280.
> Written about 1680, "Consolatory Epistle: to Julian in
his Confinement" alludes to Etherege's recent marriage:
>> Ev'n <u>gentle George</u>, with flux in <u>Tongue</u> and <u>Purse</u>,
>> In shunning <u>one snare</u> ran into a <u>worse</u>.
>> <u>Want</u> once may be reliev'd in a Mans Life,
>> But who can be reliev'd that has a Wife?
>
> <u>POAS</u>, vol. 2 (1703), p. 132, reprints the poem; but the re-
print in Buckingham, <u>Works</u> (1704), p. 20, prints a slightly
altered text. See 1928.A1. For another view by Gould, see
1709.B1.

1690

A BOOKS

1 ETHEREGE, GEORGE. <u>The Comical Revenge; or, Love in a Tub</u>.
> London: Henry Herringman, Sold by Samuel Manship. 71 pp.
> Wing E3372: W&M 549, notes that the text is the same as
1689.A1, but the title page is a cancel.

B SHORTER WRITINGS--NONE

1691

A BOOKS--NONE

B SHORTER WRITINGS

1 LANGBAINE, GERARD. <u>An Account of the English Dramatick Poets</u>.
> Oxford: L. L., for George West and Henry Clements, pp. 186-88.
> Wing L373. Praises all of Etherege's comedies: <u>Love in
a Tub</u> is of a "mixt nature" (i.e., comic and serious), <u>She
Wou'd if She Cou'd</u> should be accredited the "first rank," and
<u>The Man of Mode</u> is a "true Comedy," with "the Characters as well
drawn to the life, as any Play that has been Acted since the
Restauration of the English Stage." Langbaine concludes by
wishing that "this great Master would oblidge the World with
more of his Performances, which would put a stop to the crude
and indigested plays, which for want of better, cumber our
Stage." Two facsimile reprints: (1) Bibliography and Reference Series, no 91. (New York: Burt Franklin, [1967?].) (2)
Augustan Reprint Society, special publication (Los Angeles:
W. A. Clark Memorial Library, 1971.)

1692

A BOOKS--NONE

B SHORTER WRITINGS

1 Lacedemonian Mercury. 11 March 1691/2. Verso.
        Query 2: "Whether the Town's receiving and coveting Love
    for Money and The Marriage-Hater Match'd [comedies by Durfey,
    1691 and 1692], when at the same time The Plain Dealer and
    Sir Foplin Flutter [sic] rest untouch'd and unsought-for, be
    not Evidence of a very great declension in Common Sense?"
    See Langhans, 1973.B8; cited London Stage, 1:407 (1965.B9).

1693

A BOOKS

1 ETHEREGE, GEORGE. She Wou'd if She Cou'd. London: T. Warren,
    for H. Herringman, Sold by R. Bentley, et al., 76 pp.
        Wing E3380; W&M 557.

2 _____. The Man of Mode; or, Sir Fopling Flutter. London: T.
    Warren, for H. Herringman, Sold by R. Bentley, et al., 83 pp.
        Wing E3376; W&M 554.

B SHORTER WRITINGS

1 RYMER, THOMAS. A Short View of Tragedy. London: R. Baldwin,
    p. 160.
        Wing R2429. Probably published late 1692. Discusses
    Othello's "soft language" as he approaches Desdemona to "put
    out the light." Rymer calls this "the very Soul and Quintes-
    sence of Sir George Etherege." See 1956.B6 for a modern
    edition.

2 SOUTHERNE, THOMAS. "To Mr. Congreve." In The Old Batchelour.
    London: Peter Buck, Sig. [A3].
        Wing C5863. Remarks on Etherege in commendatory verses
    prefacing Congreve's first play.
        Loose, wandring, Etherege, in wild pleasures tost,
        And foreign Int'rests, to his hopes long lost:
    For a modern edition, see Congreve, The Complete Plays, ed.
    Herbert Davis (Chicago: University of Chicago Press, 1967),
    p. 31.

1694

A BOOKS--NONE

B SHORTER WORKS

1 DRYDEN, JOHN. "To My Dear Friend Mr. Congreve, on his Comedy,
   call'd The Double Dealer." In The Double Dealer. London:
   J. Tonson, Sig. [A₃].
      Wing C5847. Compares Congreve to other playwrights in-
   cluding Etherege:
         In Him [Congreve] all Beauties of this Age we see;
         Etherege his Courtship, Southern's Purity;
         The Satire, Wit, and Strength of Manly Witcherly.
   For a modern edition, see Congreve, The Complete Plays, ed.
   Herbert Davis (Chicago: University of Chicago Press, 1967),
   p. 123.

2 [WRIGHT, JAMES]. Country Conversations. London: Henry
   Bonwicke, pp. 1-17.
      Wing W3694. A Drydenesque discussion "Of Modern Comedies,"
   among Lisander, Julio, and Mitis, in which Mitis speaks for
   the early Restoration plays, and Julio for drama of the "last
   age." Lisander describes The Plain Dealer and Sir Fopling
   as the last truly proper comedies. Lady Cockwood is the
   prototype for a lewd wife pretending to honor, but "modern
   comedies" only copy Wycherley and Etherege.

1695

A BOOKS--NONE

B SHORTER WRITINGS

1 DRYDEN, JOHN. "Preface of the Translator." In De Arte Graphica:
   The Art of Painting by C. A. Du Fresnoy . . . Containing a
   Parallel betwixt Painting and Poetry. London: Printed by J.
   Heptinstall, for W. Rogers, p. xxxix.
      Wing D2458. "I knew a Poet, whom out of respect I will
   not name, who being too witty himself, cou'd draw nothing but
   Wits in a Comedy of his: even his Fools were infected with
   the Disease of their Author. They overflow'd with smart
   Reperties, and were only distinguish'd from the intended Wits
   by being call'd Coxcombs; though they deserv'd not so scandal-
   ous a Name." Possibly referring to Etherege. See 1962.B2.

2 SHEFFIELD, JOHN, MARQUIS OF NORMANBY. The Temple of Death. 2nd
   ed., corrected. London: Printed by T. Warren for Francis

11

1697

Saunders.
Prints a number of poems that Thorpe (1963.A1) attributes
to Etherege. Poetic remarks on Etherege in the following
expanded volumes. See 1701.B1; 1702.B2.

1697

A BOOKS

1 ETHEREGE, GEORGE. The Comical Revenge; or, Love in a Tub.
    London: T. Warren, for H. Herringman, Sold by J. Tonson, et
    al. 68 pp.
        Wing E3373; W&M 550.

2 _____. The Man of Mode; or, Sir Fopling Flutter. London: n.p.
        Wing E3377 lists copies at the British Museum and Harvard;
    W&M do not cite this edition. I could not discover a copy at
    the British Museum, now the British Library; evidentally it is
    a "ghost."

B SHORTER WRITINGS

1 ANON. "The Session of Poets." In Poems on Affairs of State.
    [London: n.p.].
        Wing P2719. Lines on Etherege and Shadwell written about
    1668:
        Eth'rege and Shadwell and the rabble appeal'd
        To Apollo himself in a very great rage,
        Because their best friends so freely had deal'd
        As totall their plays were not fit for the stage.
    Reprinted in 1963.B3.

1698

A BOOKS--NONE

B SHORTER WRITINGS

1 [SETTLE, ELKANAH.] A Defense of Dramatick Poetry. London: Eliz.
    Whitlock, pp. 84, 92-93.
        Old Wing F905. Comments that Dorimant as a stage represen-
    tation is not tempting to the audience. We laugh at him and
    that is the end of comedy. Moreover, when we see Harriet
    change Dorimant, the "reforming rover" quits his old ways for
    "a chaste Harriet."

12

1699

A BOOKS--NONE

B SHORTER WRITINGS

1 GILDON, CHARLES. Lives and Characters of the English Dramatick
    Poets. London: Tho. Leigh and William Turner. pp. 53-54.
        Wing L375. In this revision of Langbaine (1691.B1),
    Gildon alters the entry on Etherege only slightly, adding that
    the playwright was sent as "Envoy to Hamburgh [sic]." No new
    factual or critical insights on Etherege.

1701

A BOOKS--NONE

B SHORTER WRITINGS

1 SHEFFIELD, JOHN, Marquis of Normanby. A Collection of Poems:
    Viz., The Temple of Death . . . with Several Original Poems
    never before Printed. London: Printed for Daniel Brown and
    Benjamin Tooke.
        Dedicatory poem, missing from 1695.B1, praises Etherege:
    ". . . gentle Etheridge's and Sydley's Muse/Warm the Coy Maid,
    and melting Love infuse." See 1702.B2.

1702

A BOOKS--NONE

B SHORTER WRITINGS

1 DENNIS, JOHN. "Epistle Dedicatory to The Comical Gallant."
    London: A. Baldwin. Sig. [a2].
        Comments, in defense of his revision of The Merry Wives of
    Windsor, that She Wou'd if She Cou'd did not have a good open-
    ing run. Since 1668, however, "Men of Sense . . . esteem'd
    . . . the trueness of some of its Characters, and the purity
    and freshness and easie grace of its Dialogue." See Shadwell's
    earlier remarks on She Wou'd if She Cou'd, 1671.B2; for a
    modern edition of Dennis, 1939.B1, 1:289.

2 SHEFFIELD, JOHN, Marquis of Normanby. A Collection of Poems:
    Viz., The Temple of Death . . . with Several Original Poems by
    [Others]. London: Ralph Smith.
        Reprint of 1701.B1.

13

1704

A BOOKS

1 ETHEREGE, GEORGE. The Works . . . Containing his Plays and
Poems. London: for H. H., Sold by J. Tonson and T. Bennet,
288 pp.
The three plays, plus five poems, in an octavo edition.
Verity (1888.A1) uses this edition as his copytext.

B SHORTER WRITINGS--NONE

1705

A BOOKS--NONE

B SHORTER WRITINGS

1 BUCKINGHAM, GEORGE VILLIERS, DUKE OF. "A Familiar Epistle to Mr.
Julian, Secretary to the Muses." In Works. London: Sam.
Briscoe, p. 91.
Poor George grows old, his Muse worn out of Fashion;
Hoarsely he sung Ephelia's lamentation.
Refers to Etherege's poem "Ephelia to Bajazet," a verse epistle
attacking the Earl of Mulgrave, probably written in 1675.
Buckingham's couplet was probably written after Etherege's
poem and before 1677, Thorpe believes (1963.A1), pp. 79-82.
See also 1963.B3, 1:388.

1707

A BOOKS--NONE

B SHORTER WRITINGS

1 FILMER, EDWARD. A Defense of Plays. London: J. Tonson, 167 pp.
Defends plays in the wake of the Collier onslaught. Points
out Dorimant's "genteel Conversation."

1708

A BOOKS--NONE

B SHORTER WRITINGS

1 DOWNES, JOHN. Roscius Anglicanus, or an Historical Review of the
Stage . . . from 1660-1706. London: H. Playford.
Comments on Etherege's plays: "the clean and well

performance of this Comedy [Love in a Tub] got the [Duke's]
Company more Reputation and profit than any preceding Comedy;
the Company taking in a Months time at it 1000 [pounds]"; She
Wou'd if She Cou'd "took well, but inferior to Love in a Tub";
The Man of Mode "being well cloath'd and well Acted, got a
great deal of Money." Reprinted with introduction, in 1969.B3.

1709

A BOOKS--NONE

B SHORTER WRITINGS

1 GOULD, ROBERT. "The Play-house, a Satyr." In Works. 2 vols.
London: W. Lewis, 1709. 2:242.
    Revised from a poem that appeared in the 1689 volume (1689.
B1), which omits Etherege; the new version compliments Ether-
ege's work:
        The Name of Etheridge next renown'd we see
        For easy Stile, and Wit in Comedy,
        Tho' not so strong as that of Wycherley.
See 1934.B8; a modern edition with notes.

1710

A BOOKS

1 ETHEREGE, GEORGE. She Wou'd if She Cou'd. London: n.p., Printed
in the Year, 1710. 104 pp.
    Probably a piracy by Thomas Johnson. See 1711.A1; 1723.A2,
A3.

B SHORTER WORKS--NONE

1711

A BOOKS

1 ETHEREGE, GEORGE. The Man of Mode; or, Sir Fopling Flutter.
London: n.p., Printed in the Year, 1711. 112 pp.
    In the same format as 1710.A1; probably a piracy.

B SHORTER WRITINGS

1 [ADDISON, JOSEPH.] Spectator, no. 44 (20 April).
    A lengthy discussion of tragic effects in theatre con-
cludes with some remarks on comedy. Referring to Love in a
Tub, Addison says "a Lover running about the Stage, with his

1711

Head peeping out of a Barrel, was thought a very good jest in
King Charles the Second's Time; and invented by one of the
first Wits of the Age. But because Ridicule is not so delicate as Compassion, and because the Objects that make us
laugh are infinitely more numerous than those that make us
weep, there is a much greater Latitude for comick than tragick
Artifices, and by consequence a much greater Indulgence to be
allow'd them." See 1965.B7 for a modern edition with notes.
1:185-91.

2 FENTON, EL[IJAH] An Epistle to Mr. Southerne. London: B. Tooke
and B. Lintott. p. 7.
Praise of Southerne by comparing him with well-known Res-
toration playwrights, including Etherege:
When Peace and Plenty overflow'd the Land,
She strait pull'e off her Sattin Cap and Band:
Bade Witcherly be Bold in her Defence,
Glittering with pointed Wit, and manly Sense:
Etherege and Sidley join'd him in her Cause,
And all deserv'd, and all receiv'd Applause.
Reprinted in 1721.B1.

3 [STEELE, RICHARD.] Spectator, no. 51 (28 April).
Grudging remarks that it is the imaginative title of She
Wou'd if She Cou'd that attracts audiences. Nevertheless, the
play "has always been well received." Reprinted 1965.B7,
I:215-20.

4 [STEELE, RICHARD.] Spectator, no. 65 (15 May).
An attack on The Man of Mode, comparing the modes and manners of the court of Charles II with those of the court of
Queen Anne. "This celebrated piece is a perfect contradiction
to good manners, good sense, and common honesty." Dorimant
receives most of Steele's malicious criticism because of the
libertine's falsehood, deception, and barbarity, which moves
Steele to sorrow and indignation rather than laughter and
mirth. For Dennis's response, see 1722.B1, followed by
rejoinders 1722.B2, B3. Reprinted in 1965.B7, 1:278-80; 1973.
A2. The reasons for Steele's attack are considered in 1950.B4.

5 [STEELE, RICHARD.] Spectator, no. 75 (26 May).
Inveighs against anyone taking Dorimant's part, perhaps in
order to promote his own plays (see, 1950.B4). Further
criticizes The Man of Mode on moral grounds. Reprinted in
1965.B7; 1:322-25.

1715

A BOOKS

1 ETHEREGE, GEORGE. The Works, . . . Containing his Poems and Plays.
   London: Jacob Tonson, 276 pp.
      Duodecimo printing that follows the earlier collected
   plays (1704.A1). This edition, however, introduces three
   engraved plates, depicting an important scene in each of the
   plays, by Du Guernier.

B SHORTER WRITINGS

1 FELTON, HENRY. A Dissertation on Reading the Classics. 2d. ed.,
   with additions. London: Jonah Bowyer. p. 65.
      Added in this revision is praise for the classical learn-
   ing of a number of Restoration poets, including Etherege.

1716

A BOOKS--NONE

B SHORTER WRITINGS

1 SHEFFIELD, JOHN, Marquis of Normanby. "To a Very Young Lady."
   In Temple of Death. 3d ed. London: Charles Tooke.
      Reprint of poem praising Etherege. See 1701.B1; 1702.B2.

1719

A BOOKS--NONE

B SHORTER WRITINGS

1 JACOB, GILES. The Poetical Register. 2 vols. London: E. Curll,
   1:95-96, 2:265-66.
      Cites Etherege's "three excellent Comedies," giving in-
   correct dates for Love in a Tub and She Wou'd if She Cou'd,
   and mentions Etherege's "mission to Hamburgh [sic]." Compounds
   Gildon's errors; see 1699.B1. Reprinted in 1723.B1.

1720

A BOOKS--NONE

B SHORTER WRITINGS

1 [KILLIGREW, THOMAS?] Miscellanea Aurea: or The Golden Medley.

17

1721

London: for A. Bettesworth and J. Pemberton, p. 291.
Letter 9, "On The Vulgar. A Pardox": "Sir George Etherege, as great as his Reputation was, could not escape the
Reproach of Men of Judgment of his Time; one of whom says,
that he writ three talking Plays without one Plot; and yet
those three Plays are not altogether without Plot and Humour."
See 1680.B2.

1721

A BOOKS--NONE

B SHORTER WRITINGS

1 FENTON, ELIJAH. "Epistle to Mr. Southerne." In The Works of
Thomas Southerne. 2 vols. London: Tonson, et al., I, Sig.
a3v.
Reprint of 1711.B2.

1722

A BOOKS--NONE

B SHORTER WRITINGS

1 DENNIS, JOHN. A Defence of Sir Fopling Flutter. London: T.
Warner.
After quoting Aristotle on comedy's ridicule of the worst
of men, Dennis says that the comic poet exposes these men to
view in order to render them contemptible. The characters in
The Man of Mode are so drawn to give pleasure and instruct.
There follows an exposition of the characters in The Man of
Mode, and Dennis concludes by asking: "is not the proper
Business of Comedy . . . [to make] Follies and Vice ridicu-
lous?" See 1939.B1, for a modern edition of this work with
notes. Reprinted in 1973.A2, B1.

2 [STEELE, RICHARD?] "A Short Defense . . . ." In St. James
Journal, no. 29 (15 November):172-73.
Little attention given to The Man of Mode; mostly the
response is a personal attack on Dennis.

3 [DORIMANT.] St. James Journal, nos. 30 (22 November), 33 (8
December), 34 (15 December).
A writer who signs himself Dorimant undertakes a defense
of Dennis in this journal. The last and most significant
piece concludes with Pope's lines on Addison (not in their
final form). This has led some critics to ascribe these

essays to Pope. See 1722.B1, B2.

*4 VICTOR, BENJAMIN. An Epistle to Sir Richard Steele, on His Play, Call'd The Conscious Lovers. London: Chetwood, Chapman, et al.
    This response to Dennis's pamphlet (1722.B1) was advertised as "this day" published in The Evening Post no. 2081 (27-29 November). There is a review in The Freeholder's Journal, no. 50 (5 December), pp. 295-98.

1723

A BOOKS

1 ETHEREGE, GEORGE. The Works, . . . Containing his Poems and Plays. London: Jacob Tonson. 276 pp.
    "A page-for-page reprint," of 1715.A1 as Brett-Smith observes (1927.A1), though the type is new set. Also includes DuGuernier plates.

2 _____. The Man of Mode; or, Sir Fopling Flutter. London: Printed for the Company of Booksellers, n.d. 104 pp.
    The "Epilogue" is followed by a three-page list of books and plays printed by T. Johnson, The Hague, including Steele's Conscious Lovers (November 1722).

3 _____. She Wou'd if She Cou'd. London: Printed for the Company of Booksellers, n.d. 90 pp.
    Appears to be in the T. Johnson series. See 1723.A2.

B SHORTER WRITINGS

1 JACOB, GILES. The Poetical Register. 2 vols. London: E. Curll.
    Reprint of 1719.B1.

1725

A BOOKS

1 ETHEREGE, GEORGE. The Man of Mode; or, Sir Fopling Flutter.
    Dublin: Printed by S. Powell for George Risk. 89 pp.

B SHORTER WRITINGS--NONE

1733

A BOOKS

1 ETHEREGE, GEORGE. The Man of Mode; or, Sir Fopling Flutter.
   London: Printed for J. Tonson, Sold by W. Feales. 96 pp.
      Printed with Du Guerier plate. Minor variants in the
   text--"chear" for "cheer," "knaw" for "kaw," "Ambra's" for
   "Embarrass," "date" for "doat,", and "Mail" for "Mall."

B SHORTER WRITINGS--NONE

1735

A BOOKS

1 ETHEREGE, GEORGE. Works, His Plays and Poems. London: J.
   Tonson. Pagination is separate: Love in a Tub, 95 pp.; She
   Wou'd if She Cou'd, 94 pp.; The Man of Mode, 111 pp. Five
   poems included after The Man of Mode. Du Guernier plates.

1749

A BOOKS--NONE

B SHORTER WRITINGS

1 WHINCOP, THOMAS. Scanderbeg . . . To which are added, A List of
   All Dramatic Authors . . . . London: W. Reeve, p. 229.
      The "list" is usually attributed to John Mottley, who
   misdates two of the three plays. Five sentence biography.
   Probably following Jacob, see 1719.B1.

1750

A BOOKS--NONE

B SHORTER WRITINGS

1 CHETWOOD, W. R. British Theatre. Dublin: Peter Wilson. p. 81.
      Echoes Jacob (1719.B1) or Mottley (1749.B1), even to the
   mistaken dates of the plays.

2 OLDYS, WILLIAM. Biographia Britannica. 5 vols. London: W.
   Innys, et al., 1747-60. Vol. 3, covering Etherege, published
   in 1750.
      First attempt to provide a complete biographical account
   of Etherege. Talks to people who knew, or had met Etherege

--John Bowman, the actor, and Dean Lockier. On the latter
see Spence (1820.B1, 1966.B20).

1752

A BOOKS

1 ETHEREGE, GEORGE. The Man of Mode; or, Sir Fopling Flutter. In
The British Stage, Vol. 4 [of 6]. London: for J. Brindley,
104 pp.
Separate title page looks like the T. Johnson piracy. See,
1723.A2.

*2 _____. The Man of Mode; or, Sir Fopling Flutter. Dublin:
Augustus Long, n.d. 84 pp.
See Brett-Smith (1927.A1), for a discussion of this
edition, pp. ciii-civ.

1753

A BOOKS--NONE

B SHORTER WRITINGS

1 CIBBER, THEOPHILUS. Lives of the Poets of Great Britain and
Ireland. 4 vols. London: R. Griffiths. 3:33-39. [Written
on BM title page: "Compiled from MS. notes of Thomas Coxeter,
1753.]
The majority of this collection was probably done by
Robert Sheils, who seems to have based much of his material on
Oldys's biography (1750.B2). Etherege's plays are considered
"so extremely loose and licentious, as to render them danger-
ous to young unguarded minds."

1762

A BOOKS

1 ETHEREGE, GEORGE. "The French Matron." In The Matrons: Six
Short Histories. Edited by [Thomas Percy]. London: R. & J.
Dodsley, pp. 87-108.
A letter of Etherege's altered to fit a central theme.
"Edited by Thomas Percy" is written on BM copy, 12612.b.27.
Bracher reprints this letter, which he calculates was written
in March 1687, and comments on it. See 1974.A1, pp. 92-97.

B SHORTER WRITINGS--NONE

1764

1764

A BOOKS--NONE

B SHORTER WRITINGS

1 BAKER, DAVID ERSKINE. <u>The Companion to the Playhouse</u>. 2 vols.
    London: T. Becket, et al. [Vol. 1 lists plays alphabetically;
    Vol. 2 provides biographical information.]
        Notes "looseness" of the characters in <u>Love in a Tub</u>. <u>She</u>
    <u>Wou'd if She Cou'd</u>, formerly esteemed, is now laid aside. <u>The</u>
    <u>Man of Mode</u> is "perhaps the most elegant comedy, and contains
    more of the real manners of high life than any one the English
    stage was ever adorned with."

1768

A BOOKS

1 ETHEREGE, GEORGE. <u>The Man of Mode; or, Sir Fopling Flutter</u>. In
    <u>The Theatre: or Select Works of the British Dramatic Poets</u>.
    Vol. 11 [of 12]. Edinburgh: Martin and Wotherspoon, 95 pp.

B SHORTER WRITINGS--NONE

1774

A BOOKS

1 ETHEREGE, GEORGE. <u>The Man of Mode; or, Sir Fopling Flutter</u>.
    Edinburgh: J. Robertson, 95 pp.

B SHORTER WRITINGS--NONE

1778

A BOOKS

*1 ETHEREGE, GEORGE. "Plays." In <u>New British Theatre</u>. Vol. 11.
    Edinburgh: n.p. Each play paginated separately.

B SHORTER WRITINGS--NONE

1779

A BOOKS--NONE

B SHORTER WRITINGS

1 CHESTERFIELD, PHILIP STANHOPE, LORD. Letters to his Friends. 4
    vols. London: Edward and Charles Dilly, 4:363-64.
       Denounces "the monstrosity of using rimed verse as a
    vehicle of dialogue in comedy." Specifically cites Love in a
    Tub, where Etherege introduced "capital characters speaking in
    rhyme; but the public was offended at the insult offered to
    common sense."

1782

A BOOKS--NONE

B SHORTER WRITINGS

1 REED, ISAAC, and BAKER, DAVID ERSKINE. Biographia Dramatica, or
    A Companion to the Playhouse. 4 vols. London: Rivingtons,
    et al., 1:148-50; 2:61, 217-18, 338.
       Repeats Baker's information (1764.B1); Reed adds an ad-
    ditional critical remark on She Wou'd if She Cou'd from John
    Dennis (1702.B1).

1784

A BOOKS--NONE

B SHORTER WRITINGS

1 DAVIES, THOMAS. Dramatic Miscellanies. 3 vols. London: T.
    Davies, 3:169-70.
       Gives Etherege credit for being "the only dramatic writer,
    in Charles's reign, who wrote with some decency of manners and
    modesty of language . . . ."

1795

A BOOKS--NONE

B SHORTER WRITINGS

1 ANON. "Sir George Etheridge." In The European Magazine, 27
    (June 1795), 396-97.
       Reprints letter from Etherege to Dryden of 20 March 1687
    (without giving the date). See 1974.A1, pp. 102-4; 1928.A1,
    167-69.

23

1798

1798

A BOOKS--NONE

B SHORTER WRITINGS

1 WALPOLE, HORACE. "Thoughts of Comedy." In The Works. 2 vols.
     London: for Robinson and Edwards, 2:315-22.
          Written 1775 or 1776. Walpole thought The Man of Mode
     "almost the best comedy we have . . . . [It] shines as our
     first genteel comedy; the touches are natural and delicate,
     and never overcharged . . . . Less licentious conversation
     would not have painted the age." Various remarks from
     Walpole's letters reconfirm this view. See 1812.B1.

1800

A BOOKS--NONE

B SHORTER WRITINGS

1 DIBDEN, CHARLES. A Complete History of the Stage. 5 vols.
     London: for the Author, 4:117:19.
          Etherege had no principles, according to Dibden, and "his
     works are dangerous, for they are full of licentiousness."
     Certainly they are not fit for "the eye or the ears of young
     females."

1812

A BOOKS--NONE

B SHORTER WRITINGS

1 BAKER, DAVID ERSKINE; REED, ISAAC; and JONES, STEPHEN. Biograph-
     ica Dramatica; or A Companion to the Playhouse. 3 vols.
     London: Longman, et al., 1:i221-23; 2:114; 3:14-15, 264.
          Repetition of earlier work begun by Baker (1764.B1),
     continued by Reed (1782.B1), now added to by Jones, who bal-
     ances Steele's criticism of The Man of Mode (1711.B4) with
     Walpole's praise (1798.B1).

2 [COLERIDGE, SAMUEL TAYLOR.] "Sir George Etherege, &c." In
     Omniana, or Horae Otiosiores. 2 vols. London: Longman, et
     al. 2:20-28.
          The difference between reading and seeing a play is that
     the grossness is often brought out in the latter. Despite
     the vulgarity he finds, Coleridge goes on to quote a scene

from <u>Love in a Tub</u> (III.iv). Reprinted in 1836.B1.

3 R. E. R. "Letter of 17 Nov." <u>Gentleman's Magazine</u> 82, ii:608.
    Points out the inconsistency of the author of <u>Omniana</u>
    (1812.B2), who condemns the grossness of the language and the
    indelicacy of the action, while eulogizing the wit and humor
    of Etherege's <u>Love in a Tub</u>.

1818

A BOOKS--NONE

B SHORTER WRITINGS

1 EVELYN, JOHN. <u>Memoirs</u>. 2 vols. Edited by William Bray. London:
    Henry Colburn, 1:348.
    Bray's selections (February to May 1664) omit Evelyn's
    attendance of <u>Love in a Tub</u>.

1819

A BOOKS--NONE

B SHORTER WRITINGS

1 HAZLITT, WILLIAM. "On Cowley, Butler, Suckling, Etherege, etc."
    Lecture 3 in <u>Lectures on the English Comic Writers</u>. (Deliv-
    ered at the Surr[e]y Institution.) London: Taylor & Hessey,
    pp. 92-132, especially pp. 129-32.
    Hazlitt calls <u>The Man of Mode</u> "a more exquisite and airy
    picture of the manners of that age than any other extant," and
    wishes that the play could be revived with Mr. Liston as Sir
    Fopling.

1820

A BOOKS--NONE

B SHORTER WRITINGS

1 SPENCE, JOSEPH. <u>Observations, Anecdotes, and Characters of Books
    and Men</u>. Edited by S. W. Singer. London: W. H. Carpenter.
    Interviews with various people (Dean Lockier, Pope, and
    Cibber) about their knowledge of writers and poets they had
    known, including Etherege. Reprinted in 1966.B20.

1822

1822

A BOOKS--NONE

B SHORTER WRITINGS

1 LAMB, CHARLES. "On the Artificial Comedy of the Last Century."
   London Magazine (April).
      In this piece, one of three "On Some of the Old Actors,"
   Lamb states that "Dorimants" do not offend his moral sense,
   but The Man of Mode is not discussed at all. See 1943.B1;
   1979.B4.

1823

A BOOKS--NONE

B SHORTER WRITINGS

1 LAMB, CHARLES. Essays of Elia. London: Taylor and Hessy.
      Reprint of 1822.B1, as well as the other essays in the
   series "On . . . Old Actors." See 1943.B1; 1979.B4. Reprinted in 1973.A2.

1824

A BOOKS--NONE

B SHORTER WRITINGS

1 HOOD, EU[GENE]. Gentleman's Magazine 95:392.
      Explains the reference to Cully's dancing "Barnaby" in
   Love in a Tub (V. ii.29), "an old dance to a quick movement,"
   as coming from Braithwait's famous Drunken Barnaby. Cites a
   Pepysian Ballad of 1655 to show the dance's popularity.

1825

A BOOKS--NONE

B SHORTER WRITINGS

1 PEPYS, SAMUEL. Memoirs. 2 vols. Deciphered by the Rev. John
   Smith. Edited by Richard, Lord Braybrooks. London: Henry
   Colburn.
      Includes some entires concerning Pepy's reactions to
   Etherege's plays.

1826

A BOOKS--NONE

B SHORTER WRITINGS

1 NORTH, ROGER. "Life of Lord Keeper Guildford." In Lives of the
   Norths. 2 vols. London: Henry Colburn, 2:232-34.
       Cites an actual event that is "the very action which Mr.
   Etheredge describes in his play of 'Love in a Tub.'" Charles
   Crompton, like Nicholas Cully, is conned into a duel which is
   dropped when an "acquittance" is signed upon a cheat's back
   in the field.

1832

A BOOKS--NONE

B SHORTER WRITINGS

1 GENEST, JOHN. Some Account of the English Stage from the Restoration in 1660 to 1830. 10 vols. Bath: for H. E.
   Carrington, passim.
       Lists performance dates, cast lists of original presenta-
   tion, plot summaries, and comments on many plays and playwrights, including Etherege.

1836

A BOOKS--NONE

B SHORTER WRITINGS

1 COLERIDGE, SAMUEL TAYLOR. "Sir George Etherege, &c." In
   Literary Remains. 4 vols. Ed. Hartley Coleridge. London:
   William Pickering, 1836-39. 1:330-35.
       Reprint of 1812.B2.

1838

A BOOKS--NONE

B SHORTER WRITINGS

1 [DUNHAM, SAMUEL A.] Eminent Literary and Scientific Men of Great
   Britain and Ireland. In The Cabinet Cyclopaedia. 3 vols.
   London: Longman, et al. 3:175-82.
       The "prurient plots and lacivious dialogues" are carried

1841

on "with the most captivating charms of language." The Man
of Mode, "the most careful of his plays," has "more real
nature . . . than in either of the former." Dunham cites
Steele as the major critic on Etherege, and agrees with the
Spectator papers (See 1711.B4).

1841

A BOOKS--NONE

B SHORTER WRITINGS

1 MACAULAY, THOMAS BABBINGTON. "Comic Dramatists of the Restora-
     tion." Edinburgh Review 72:490-528.
         Review of Leigh Hunt's edition of Wycherley, Congreve,
     Vanbrugh, and Farquhar. Only a brief mention of Etherege.
     Reprinted in 1898.B1.

1852

A BOOKS--NONE

B SHORTER WRITINGS

1 RUGGE, THOMAS. "Etherege." In "Contemporary Notes for a History
     of England Between 1659 and 1672." Edited by Peter Cunningham
     from BM Add. Mss. 10116 and 10117. Gentleman's Magazine, n.s.
     38 (July):52.
         A contemporary diary entry on Etherege's going as secretary
     to Sir Daniel Harvey, the newly appointed ambassador, to
     Turkey in August 1668.

1856

A BOOKS--NONE

B SHORTER WRITINGS

1 HETTNER, HERMAN. Geschichte de Englischen Literatur von der
     Weiderherstellung des Königthums bis in die zweite Halfte des
     achtzehnten Jahrhunderts: 1660-1700. Braunschweig:
     Friedrich Bieweg, p. 110.
         Early German literary history of England. Only one para-
     graph devoted to Etherege: mentions his friendship with
     Dorset, Rochester, and Buckingham; lists his three plays; and
     notes that the plays are lusty and spirited, but not for the
     average reader.

1857

A BOOKS--NONE

B SHORTER WRITINGS

1 FORGUES, E.-D. "John Wilmot, Comte de Rochester." Revue des
   Deux Mondes 2 (July-August):822-62; 2 (Sept-October), 144-87.
   Working from Pepys, St. Evremond, and Grammount, Forgues
   treats the life of Rochester, including a longish discussion
   on The Man of Mode, in which Rochester is cast as Dorimant
   and Sedley as Medley. Most of the exposition (pp. 840-48), of
   The Man of Mode shows how clever and witty Rochester (Dorimant)
   is.

2 LUTTRELL, NARSISSIS. A Brief Historical Relation of State Affairs
   from September 1678 to April 1714. 6 vols. Oxford: Oxford
   University Press, 2:171.
   Under February 1690/1: "Those from France say . . . that
   Sir George Etherege, the late King James ambassador to Vienna
   [sic], died lately at Paris."

1864

A BOOKS--NONE

B SHORTER WRITINGS

1 ANON. "Scottish Religious Houses Abroad." Edinburgh Review 119
   (January):168-202.
   Brief mention of Abbot Fleming's career as head of the St.
   Jacob Benedictine Abbey at Ratisbon. Remarks that Etherege
   left a "library of valuable books" to the monastery.

2 DORAN, DR. [JOHN]. "Their Majesties Servants." In Annals of the
   English Stage from Thomas Betterton to Edmund Kean. 2 vols.
   London: William H. Allen, 1:187-92.
   A Macaulayesque treatment of the "licentious" Etherege,
   including remarks from Pepys (1825.B1), Downes (1708.B1),
   Steele (1711.B4), and Dennis (1722.B1). Although Doran does
   allow the plays an amount of "bustle and succession of incidents," he leaves the plays "with a feeling of a strong want
   of purification." Reprinted revision in 1888.B1.

3 TAINE, H. Histoire de literatur du angleterre. 2 vols. Paris:
   n.p., 1:337.
   More attention to misinformation about Etherege's life
   than his works. See 1871.B1.

1866

A BOOKS--NONE

B SHORTER WRITINGS

1 BELL, ROBERT. "The Comedies of Etherege." <u>Fortnightly Review</u>
3:298-316.
Admiration for Etherege's handling of plot and dialogue.
<u>Love in a Tub</u> is successful on stage, though difficult to
follow because of its four plots; whereas <u>She Wou'd if She</u>
<u>Cou'd</u> is intrigue from first to last, yet not as successful on
stage. Only <u>The Man of Mode</u>, Etherege's "finest achievement,
. . . is sustained with unflagging energy and spirit." Unusu-
ally enthusiastic article for its day.

1871

A BOOKS--NONE

B SHORTER WRITINGS

1 TAINE, H. <u>History of English Literature</u>. 2 vols. Translated by
H. Van Laun. Edinburgh: Edmonston and Douglas, 1:479-80.
Translation of 1864.B3. "Etheredge is the first to set
the example of imitative comedy in his <u>Man of Fashion [sic]</u>."
Attacks Etherege's roistering ways.

1875

A BOOKS--NONE

B SHORTER WRITINGS

1 WARD, ADOLPHUS WILLIAM. <u>A History of English Dramatic Literature</u>
<u>to the Death of Queen Anne</u>. 2 vols. London: Macmillan,
2:566-67.
Charges Etherege with "appealing . . . to the worst tastes
of his own age." <u>Love in a Tub</u> and <u>She Wou'd if She Cou'd</u>
are "grotesque," but Ward allows some merit to <u>The Man of Mode</u>.
See Revision 1899.B2.

1876

A BOOKS--NONE

1878

B SHORTER WRITINGS

1 BELJAME, ALEXANDRE. "Sir George Etherege (1636-1689)." Notes and Queries 54:196.
     Answer to 1876.B3. Early sources on Etherege's life are Biographia Britannica (1750.B2) and Spence's Anecdotes (1820. B1).

2 BROOKE, STOPFORD. English Literature. London: Macmillan, p. 114.
     Yokes Etherege with other early Restoration dramatists, especially Wycherley and Behn. Calls the wit in the plays "vulgar and licentious."

3 FRAENATUS. [pseud.]. "Sir George Etherege (1636-1689)." Notes and Queries 54:48.
     Desires references to early sources about Etherege's life for a biography. Answered in 1876.B1.

1878

A BOOKS--NONE

B SHORTER WRITINGS

1 GRISY, A. de. Histoire de la Comédie Anglaise au Dix-Septième Siècle: 1672-1707. Paris: Didier, p. 40.
     Using Leigh Hunt's edition of the Restoration playwrights, which omits Etherege, Grisy makes only one brief mention, saying that Etherege was out of fashion.

2 HATTON, CHARLES. "Letter of 29 June 1676." Hatton Family Correspondence. 2 vols. Edited by M. Thompson. Camden Society, n.s. 22. London: Camden Society, 1:133-34.
     Describes the episode at Epsom in which Rochester, Etherege, and Captain Bridges [or possibly William Jepson] were involved. What started as a joke, ended in the death of Mr. Downs. Brett-Smith (1927.A1) quotes the letter in full, pp. xxvi-xxvii.

3 _____. "Letter of 15 Jan 1679/80." Hatton Family Correspondence. 2 vols. Edited by M. Thompson. Camden Society, n.s. 22. London: Camden Society, 1:216.
     Reports the fall of a tennis court roof which injured Sir Charles Sedley, Sir George Etherege, and others. First mention of Etherege's knighthood.

1879

A BOOKS--NONE

B SHORTER WRITINGS

1 EVELYN, JOHN. Diary. 4 vols. Edited by William Bray, with a
    life by H. B. Wheatley. London: Bickers and Son, 2:164.
        On 27 April 1664, Evelyn saw Love in a Tub, "a facetious
    comedy."

1881

A BOOKS--NONE

B SHORTER WRITINGS

1 BELJAME, ALEXANDRE. Le public et les hommes de lettres en
    Angleterre au XVIIIe siècle (1660-1744). Paris: Hachette.
        Generally disapproves of the naughty plays by Etherege.
    Translated in 1948.B1.

2 GOSSE, EDMUND. "Sir George Etheredge: A Neglected Chapter of
    English Literature." Cornhill Magazine 43 (March):284-304.
        Sees the plays as a "faithful picture . . . of fashionable
    life." We can dispense with the serious plot of Love in a Tub
    and concentrate on the "gay, realistic scenes which give the
    play its sub-title 'Tale of a Tub' [sic]." First extensive use
    of the Letterbook (edited in 1928.A1). A strong reappraisal.
    Reprinted in 1883.B1; 1885.B1; 1897.B1.

1882

A BOOKS--NONE

B SHORTER WRITINGS

1 FITZGERALD, PERCY. A New History of the English Stage. 2 vols.
    London: Tinsley Bros., 1:187-88.
        Mentions only The Man of Mode; from "Sir Fopling may be
    traced the groundwork of almost all the Foppington and petit-
    maîtres which appeared in the succeeding comedies of that
    period."

1883

A BOOKS--NONE

B SHORTER WRITINGS

1 GOSSE, EDMUND. "Sir George Etheredge." In Seventeenth-Century
Studies. London: Kegan Paul, Trench, pp. 231-65.
Reprint of 1881.B2.

A BOOKS--NONE

B SHORTER WRITINGS

1 GOSSE, EDMUND. "Sir George Etheredge." In Seventeenth-Century
Studies. London: Kegan Paul, Trench, pp. 231-65.
Reprint of 1881.B2; 1883.B1.

2 STEPHEN, LESLIE. "Sir George Etherege." In Dictionary of National Biography. London: Smith & Elder, 6:908.
An unsympathetic treatment of Etherege the man. Stephen
does admit, however, that "Etherege was clever in catching
the fashions of the day."

A BOOKS

1 ETHEREGE, GEORGE. The Works of Sir George Etheredge: Plays and
Poems. Edited by A. W. Verity. London: John C. Nimmo, xxxi
+ 408 pp.
Copytext is 1704.A1, the first collected edition. A brief
account of the life is followed by a review of the plays,
pointing out that Etherege's repartee comedy differs from
humours comedy. Reviewed in Athenaeum, no. 3179 (29 September), pp. 409-11. Reprinted in 1975.A2; 1977.A1.

B SHORTER WRITINGS

*1 DORAN, J. Annals of the English Stage from Thomas Betterton to
Edmund Kean. Edited and revised by Robert W. Lowe. 2 vols.
London: John C. Nimmo.
See 1864.B2. Portion on Etherege may be revised.

2 MARSHALL, JULIAN. Notes and Queries, 7th ser., no. 7 (18
February), p. 135.
Answers query of 4 February (p. 89) about "Flute doux" in
The Man of Mode. But the explanation of "Diversions of
Bruxells" is unanswered. For the latter, see Cox (1968.B5).

33

1893

1893

A BOOKS--NONE

B SHORTER WRITINGS

1 PEPYS, SAMUEL. The Diary. 10 vols. Edited by H. B. Wheatley.
   London: G. Bell, 1893-98.
        4 January 1664/5 (Love in a Tub): 4:325; 29 October 1666
   (Love in a Tub): 6:43; 6 February 1667/8 (She Wou'd if She
   Cou'd): 7:306-308; 29 April 1668 (Love in a Tub): 7:413; 1
   February 1668/9 (She Wou'd if She Cou'd): 8:215-17. See
   Revision in 1968.B15.

2 STREET, GEORGE S. "Etherege." In Minatures and Moods. London:
   Nutt, pp. 34-39.
        Provides a brief discussion on the three plays. Concludes
   that Etherege is notable "for an effective restraint in
   satire."

3 VERITY, A. W. In Athenaeum, no. 3426 (24 June), p. 808.
        On a trip to Ratisbon, Verity was able to find no papers
   of Etherege in the Schotten Kloster, but he did discover
   eight books with the entry "Left by Sir George Etherege with
   Abbot Fleming."

1896

A BOOKS--NONE

B SHORTER WRITINGS

1 BATES, KATHERINE LEE, and GODFREY, LYDIA BOKER. English Drama:
   A Working Bibliography. Wellesley, Mass.: Wellesley College,
   p. 98.
        Described by Ms. Bates [on the BL copy--011904. ee. 12] as
   "Hastily compiled and privately printed for class use with the
   hope . . . of later revision and publication." Brief, but
   inclusive, primary and secondary checklist for playwrights
   including Etherege.

1897

A BOOKS--NONE

B SHORTER WRITINGS

1 GOSSE, EDMUND. "Sir George Etheredge." In Seventeenth-Century

34

Studies. London: Heinemann; New York: Dodd, Mead, pp. 259-
98.
    Reprint of 1881.B2 (essay) and 1883.B1 (book). Adds a
footnote on Stadt-am-hof [Bayrischenhof] and mentions Verity's
edition (1888.A1) in the foreword.

<u>1898</u>

A BOOKS--NONE

B SHORTER WRITINGS

1 MACAULAY, THOMAS BABBINGTON. <u>Works</u>. London: Longman-Green, p.
    338f.
        Reprint of 1841.B1.

2 PRIDEAUX, W. F. "Sir George Etheredge," <u>Notes and Queries</u> 97:
    365.
        Recalls Cunningham's mention of Rugge's diary (1852.B1) on
    Etherege's departure for Turkey. Also notes that the 1664
    edition of <u>Love in a Tub</u> is not as scarce as Verity (1888.A1)
    thought: both Prideaux and Edmund Gosse have copies.

<u>1899</u>

A BOOKS--NONE

B SHORTER WRITINGS

*1 TAYLOR, EMERSON G. "The Influence of French Comedy on English
    Comedy of the late Seventeenth Century." Dissertation, Yale
    University.
        Cited in McNamee.

2 WARD, ADOLPHUS WILLIAM. <u>A History of English Dramatic Literature
    to the Death of Queen Anne</u>, 2d ed. 3 vols. London:
    Macmillan, 3:442-46.
        In this revision of an earlier work (1875.B1), Ward--
    doubtlessly influenced by Gosse's essay (1881.B2) and Verity's
    edition (1888.A1)--gives Etherege's work much more attention
    here than in his previous survey. <u>Love in a Tub</u>, with its
    mixture of verse and prose, succeeds because of the realism
    of the prose scenes. <u>She Wou'd if She Cou'd</u>, "a distinct
    advance upon its precedessor," is commended for "the ease and
    brightness of the dialogues." In <u>The Man of Mode</u>, Etherege
    reaches "his high point of excellence as a comic writer,"
    because "the humour of his conception [is kept] within
    bounds."

1900

1900

A BOOKS

*1 WÜRZBACH-TANNENBERG, ALFRED RITTER von, Jr. George Etheredge.
   Leipzig: O. R. Reisland.
       RECTR: "first characteristically Restoration dramatist,
   prepared the way for the more able playwrights, Wycherley,
   Congreve, and Farquhar. Part I biography; part II discussion
   of the plays." (I was unable to locate this book. The
   British Museum catalogue gives an Alfred Wolfgang von Würzbach
   and a Constant Von Tannenberg Würzbach--see 1900.B1.)

B SHORTER WRITINGS

1 WÜRZBACH, WOLFGANG von. "George Etheredge." Englische Studien
   27:234-52.
       The first part of this essay (pp. 234-41) covers the known
   facts of Sir George's life. The second part (pp. 242-52)
   treats each of the plays in order (Love in a Tub, 242-45; She
   Wou'd if She Cou'd, 245-48; The Man of Mode, 248-52). More
   plot summaries than analyses.

1901

A BOOKS

1 MEINDL, VINCENZ. Sir George Etheredge, Sein Leben, Seine Zeit
   und Seine Dramen. Wiener Beiträge zur englischen Philologie,
   no. 14. Wien and Leipzig: Braumüller, 278 pp.
       After listing his sources, Meindl writes a biography of
   Etherege (pp. 3-101). The next part (pp. 102-36) takes up
   the Restoration stage before handling each of the plays in
   turn (Love in a Tub, pp. 136-72; She Wou'd if She Cou'd, pp.
   172-200; The Man of Mode, pp. 200-238). After a review of
   previous criticism (pp. 238-52), Meindl sums up his subject,
   for whom he has mixed feelings. In the end, Meindl does allow
   Etherege occasional merit: the plays are often lively and the
   dialogue sometimes clever. Reviewed by Richard Ackerman,
   Beiblatt zur Anglia, 14 (1903):133-7. Reprinted in 1964.A2.

B SHORTER WRITINGS--NONE

1902

A BOOKS--NONE

36

B SHORTER WRITINGS

1 [LONGUEVILLE, THOMAS.] <u>Rochester and other Literary Rakes</u>.
London: Longmans Green, pp. 108-16.
   A repeat of stale sources (Oldys, 1750.B2) for Edwardian
consumption. The author condemns Etherege while telling his
story with relish.

1903

A BOOKS--NONE

B SHORTER WRITINGS

1 PERWICH, WILLIAM. <u>Despatches of William Perwich, English Agent
in Paris, 1669-1677</u>. Edited by M. Beryl Curran. Camdem
Series, Vol. 5, no. 3. London: Royal Historical Society,
pp. 77-78.
   Perwich to William Blathwayt at the Hague: [1 May 1671]
"If Mr. Woseley be there I pray administer my humble service
to him & tell him Etheridge that made Love in a Tub is here
[Paris] & contributes extremely to our divertisement." Noted
by Brett-Smith (1927.A1), p. xx; the original letter, former-
ly in the possession of G. Thorn-Drury, is now lost.

1906

A BOOKS--NONE

B SHORTER WRITINGS

1 ANDERSON, P.J., ed. <u>Records of the Scots Colleges at Douai,
Rome, Madrid, Valladolid, and Ratisbon</u>. Aberdeen: New
Spalding Club, p. 275.
   Cites Etherege as a benefactor of the Scottish Monastery
Library at Ratisbon. Also notes Etherege's death as a
Catholic at Paris on 28 July 1699, corrected to 1694.

2 CHARLANNE, L[OUIS]. <u>L'Influence Française en Angleterre au
XVIIe Siècle: Le Théâtre et la Critique</u>. Paris: Société
Française, pp. 300-302.
   Believes Etherege picked up "La Vengeance Comique" from
Molière. Gosse (1881.B2) is cited as his authority for con-
necting the two dramatists.

3 HARVEY-JELLIE, W. <u>Les Sources du théâtre Anglais a l'epoque de
la restauration</u>. Paris: Librairie Générale, pp. 59-63.
   Gives Etherege the credit for the first use of the heroic

1907

couplet in the drama and for introducing modern comedy with
Love in a Tub, which assimilates the spirit of Molière. Lady
Cockwood, in She Wou'd if She Cou'd, is a female Tartuffe, and
The Man of Mode has an intellectual resemblance to Molière's
late comedies.

<u>1907</u>

A BOOKS--NONE

B SHORTER WRITINGS

1 KERBY, W. MOSELEY. Molière and Restoration Comedy in England.
   Rennes: n.p. pp. 24-9.
        Points out what are considered parallels: Tartuffe with
   Sir Fopling; Dufoy with Mascarille in L'Etourdi; and Lady
   Cockwood as a female Tartuffe.

2 MUDDYMAN, JOHN. "Letter to John Wilmot, Earl of Rochester."
   Historical Manuscripts Commission Calendar of the Manuscripts
   of the Marquis of Bath. 2 vols. Dublin: HM Stationery Office, by John Falconer, 2:153.
        [September, 1671]: "This side [of the page] shall carry
   you within the rayles of Covent Garden where you shall behold
   the furious combat of Ashton and Etherege, which ended happily
   in a fall on Ashton's part--company interposing and not suf-
   fering um to renew fight."

3 SAVILE, HENRY. "Letter to the Earl of Rochester." Historical
   Manuscripts Commission Calendar of the Manuscripts of the
   Marquis of Bath. 2 vols. Dublin: HM Stationery Office, by
   John Falconer, 2:160.
        Refers to Fleetwood Shepheard's attempt to break up a
   tavern brawl between Etherege and Henry Buckley, the conten-
   tious Master of the King's Household in November 1677. See
   1941.B1 for an annotated edition.

<u>1910</u>

A BOOKS--NONE

B SHORTER WRITINGS

1 MILES, DUDLEY HOWE. The Influence of Molière on Restoration
   Comedy. New York: Columbia University Press, pp. 61-68,
   135-39, 178-82.
        Discusses general influence on Etherege (pp. 61-68), close
   parallels (pp. 135-39), and similarities in dialogue (pp.

178-82).

2 [GOSSE, EDMUND.] "Sir George Etherege." Encyclopaedia Britannica, 11th ed. London: Encyclopaedia Britannica, 9:807.
A trimmed version of Gosse's essay (1181.B2); reprinted
in 1883.B1; 1885.B1; 1897.B1. In the 1913.B2 reprint, Gosse
owns that he wrote this entry.

1912

A BOOKS--NONE

B SHORTER WRITINGS

1 SCHELLING, FELIX E. "The Restoration Drama, I." In The Age of
Dryden. Edited by A. W. Ward and A. R. Waller. Vol. 8 of
The Cambridge History of English Literature. Cambridge:
Cambridge University Press; New York: G. P. Putnam pp. 136-39.
Etherege is a writer of "spirit, gaiety, and brillancy in
the prose dialogue of his comedies." Etherege's subjects are
"men of quality who can fight at need with spirit and verve,
but whose customary occupation is the pursuit of pleasure
without dignity and without reflection." [Quoted in Schelling].
Etherege, he concludes, captured the nature of his society.

1913

A BOOKS--NONE

B SHORTER WRITINGS

1 GILLET, J. E. Molière en Angleterre, 1660-1670. Memoires de
l'Academie Royal de Belgique, second series, vol. 9. Bruxel-
les: Hayez, pp. 33-9, 64-70.
Finds the principal parallels of Dufoy to be Mascarille in
l'Etourdi, le Depit amoureux, and les Precieuses ridicules
(pp. 33-9). Despite the alleged borrowings, Etherege earns
praise for his characters, milieu, and language in Love in a
Tub. She Wou'd if She Cou'd is an intelligent adaptation of
Molière.

2 GOSSE, EDMUND. "Sir George Etheredge." In Seventeenth-Century
Studies. London: Heinemann, pp. 259-98.
Reprint of 1897.B1. See also 1881.B2; 1883.B1; 1885.B1;
1910.B2.

3 PALMER, JOHN. "The Life and the Plays of Sir George Etherege."
In The Comedy of Manners. London: G. Bell, (chapters 2 & 3)

1913

pp. 30-91.
Claims three reasons for Etherege's importance: 1) his
use of heroic couplets rather than blank verse, 2) his stylistic elegance, 3) his foundation of "the comedy of manners."
Palmer praises the dialogue of all three plays but singles out
The Man of Mode as the essential comedy of manners. "Etherege
was a perfect opportunist, which explains why he was able to
grow old without losing his character, and turn from play-
writing to diplomacy in middle life." Portions reprinted in
1973.A2.

*4 STRUVE, JUERGEN. Das Traummotiv in Englischen Drama des XVII.
Jahrhunderts. Heidelberg: Carl Winter, xiv +104 pp.
In McNamee.

1914

A BOOKS--NONE

B SHORTER WRITINGS

1 NETTLETON, GEORGE H. English Drama of the Restoration and
Eighteenth Century (1642-1780). New York: Macmillan, pp. 73-
77.
Comments that the plays of Etherege are weak in plot and
action but strong in dialogue and laughter. Remarks that
Hunt's omission of Etherege in his 1840 collection may have
slowed Etherege's dramatic recognition. Reprinted in 1921.B2;
1923.B2; 1928.B6; 1932.B2; 1968.B14.

2 SCHELLING, FELIX E. "Dryden and the Drama of the Restoration."
In English Drama. London: Dent; New York: Dutton, pp. 234-
69, especially pp. 259f.
A condensation of his earlier essay in CHEL (1912.B1).
Little is said of the plays, more about Etherege's profligate
habits. Schelling does concede Etherege's originality, but
adds "Etherege copied the life he knew, [and] his successors
copied Etherege."

1916

A BOOKS--NONE

B SHORTER WRITINGS

1 McAFEE, H. Pepys on the Restoration Stage. New Haven: Yale
University Press, pp. 157-59.
Etherege from the point of view of Pepys. See also

40

1665.B1; 1666.B1; 1668.B1; 1668.B2; 1669.B1; and the collected
diaries 1825.B1; 1893.B1; 1968.B15.

2 MILES, DUDLEY H. "Morals of the Restoration." Sewanee Review,
24 (January):105-14.
   In response to Palmer (1913.B3) and Nettleton (1914.B1),
Miles argues that the purposes of the writers of Restoration
comedy were not to enjoin morality, but to be as witty as
possible. Wit was the "passport" of the fine gentlemen of the
town. Love in a Tub set forth the ruling passion of wit for
the remainder of the century.

1920

A BOOKS--NONE

B SHORTER WRITINGS

1 ABBOTT, G. F. Under the Turk in Constantinople: A Record of
Sir John Finch's Embassy, 1674-1681. London: Macmillan,
passim.
   Gives Etherege strong support as a diplomat: "The one
letter from him on Turkish affairs and personalities preserved
at the Public Record Office makes us wish for more; a better
informed or better written document does not exist in all the
Turkish State Papers." For the letter, see Bracher (1974.A1),
pp. 3-6. See 1921.B1; 1956.B3.

1921

A BOOKS--NONE

B SHORTER WRITINGS

1 ISAACS, J. "Sir George Etherege at Constantinople." TLS, 10
November, p. 734.
   Mentions Etherege's letter from Turkey (1971.A1, pp. 3-6),
and tries to determine when he returned to England, certainly
before the fight with Ashton in September 1671 (see, 1907.B2).
Minor correspondence following in TLS, 17 November, p. 752;
24 November, p. 771; 1 December, pp. 788-89.

2 NETTLETON, GEORGE H. English Drama of the Restoration and
Eighteenth Century (1642-1780). New York: Macmillan, pp. 73-
77.
   Reprint of 1914.B1.

3 WAINEWRIGHT, JOHN B. "George Etherege." Notes and Queries

1922

141:506.
Wishes to know if the dramatist, Sir George Etherege, belonged to the family of George Etherege, Regius Professor of Greek at Oxford University in the late sixteenth century.

1922

A BOOKS--NONE

B SHORTER WRITINGS

1 FOSTER, DOROTHY. "Concerning the Grandfather and Father of Sir George Etherege." Notes and Queries, 142:341-44, 362-65.
A two-part article on the playwright's relations and their investments in the Virginia and Bermuda companies. Part two focuses on Sir George's father, his law suits, and his activities. See also 1922.B2.

2 _____. "Concerning the Grandfather and Father of Sir George Etherege: Addenda et Corrigenda." Notes and Queries 142:414.
Some corrections and additions to 1922.B1.

3 _____. "Sir George Etherege, I." TLS, 16 February, p. 108.
Mentions law suits of the playwright, includes a genealogy (superseded by 1928.B3), and cites some poems in manuscript on Sir George's marriage.

4 _____. "Sir George Etherege, II." TLS, 23 February, p. 124.
Cites 1) contemporary anecdotes about Etherege, 2) records Etherege's financial arrangements at Ratisbon, 3) quotes two letters in full, not found in the letterbook. See Bracher (1974.A1), pp. 11-12 (3 December 1685) and pp. 79-80 (11 January 1687).

5 HELDT, W. "A Chronological and Critical Review of the Appreciation and Condemnation of the Comic Dramatists of the Restoration and Orange Periods." Neophilologus 8 (1922-3):39-59; 109-28; 197-204.
A three-part article reviewing scholarship on Restoration comedy. Etherege is clearly the villain of the piece: "his comedies we consider as a faithful reflection of these unmoral times . . . all these [Restoration] plays (except those of Etherege) were written on a moral plan . . ."

6 SWAEN, A. E. H. "Sir George Etherege." TLS, 5 January, p. 13.
Fails to discover any evidence of Etherege's residence in The Hague in 1685.

Writings by and about Etherege

1923

A BOOKS

1 ETHEREGE, GEORGE. The Man of Mode; or, Sir Fopling Flutter. In
Types of English Drama, 1660-1780. Edited by David Harrison
Stevens. Boston: Ginn, pp. 30-79.
No introduction.

B SHORTER WRITINGS

1 ARCHER, WILLIAM. The Old Drama and the New: An Essay in Re-
Valuation. London: Heinemann; Boston: Small, Maynard, pp.
172-202.
Questions the moral and aesthetic success of Restoration
comedy. About Love in a Tub, Archer remarks, "there is . . .
no trace of anything that can be called artistry either in
the invention or in the ordering of the incidents." He condemns the plays as immoral, and like L. C. Knights after him
(1937.B1), says they are not very good plays.

2 NETTLETON, GEORGE H. English Drama of the Restoration and
Eighteenth Century (1642-1780). New York: Macmillan, pp.
73-77.
Reprint of 1914.B1.

3 NICOLL, ALLARDYCE. A History of Restoration Drama. Cambridge:
Cambridge University Press, pp. 234-37, passim.
High praise for the comedies of Etherege: although Love
in a Tub is a "tentative effort," She Wou'd if She Cou'd has
got "the new age . . . fairly started." With The Man of Mode,
"the comedy of manners came to its majority." Reprinted in
1928.B7; 1940.B4; 1952.B4.

1924

A BOOKS--NONE

B SHORTER WRITINGS

1 CHANCELLOR, EDWIN BERESFORD. Lives of the Rakes. 2 vols.
London: P. Allan, 2:117-56.
Biography based on existing sources.

2 DOBRÉE, BONAMY. "Etherege." In Restoration Comedy, 1660-1720.
Oxford: Clarendon Press, pp. 58-77.
Ambivalent about Etherege's contribution to Restoration
comedy: Love in a Tub "need not be taken very seriously"; She

1924

<u>Wou'd if She Cou'd</u> is like a ballet, but not well conceived; and while Sir Fopling is a delight, the Dorimant-Loveit scenes are too cruel. Thus, Etherege "is a minor writer," whose plays have no depth at all. Much critical revaluation of Dobrée's position has taken place since 1950. Reprinted in 1938.B1; 1946.B1; 1951.B2; 1955.B4; 1858.B4; 1962.B1; 1970.B5.

3 KRUTCH, JOSEPH WOOD. <u>Comedy and Conscience after the Restoration</u>. New York: Columbia University Press, pp. 18-19, 174-76, passim.

Treats the convergence of literature and morals in the period. <u>Love in a Tub</u>, he considers "old fashioned: it might have been written before the civil war"; <u>She Wou'd if She Cou'd</u> is more concerned with a "series of polite intrigues"; <u>The Man of Mode</u> is based only on contemporary manners. Reprinted (with index and updated bibliography by G. S. Alleman) in 1949.B1; 1961.B3; 1969.B7.

*4 LYNCH, KATHLEEN M. "English Sources of Restoration Comedy of Manners." Dissertation, University of Michigan.

In McNamee; see book 1926.B3.

5 STOLL, ELMER EDGAR. "Literature No 'Document.'" <u>Modern Language Review</u> 19:141-57.

Plays of the Restoration do not represent real life, and they, therefore, cannot be taken as social documents. "Comedy is ever in league with nature, and not virtue." He cites an interchange between Dorimant and Loveit by way of example.

*6 WEISS, ADOLF. "Die Mundart im Englischen Drama von 1642-1800." Dissertation, Giessen.

In McNamee.

<u>1925</u>

A BOOKS--NONE

B SHORTER WRITINGS

1 DOBRÉE, BONAMY. "His Excellency Sir George Etherege." In <u>Essays in Biography, 1680-1726</u>. London: Oxford University Press, pp. 1-56.

Though clearly an improvement over Chancellor (1924.B1), Dobrée's biography of Etherege focuses on the years at Ratisbon, using the letterbook as the principal source. Reprinted in 1967.B5.

*2 FROHBERG, GEORG. "Das Fortleben des Elisabethanischen Drama im

Zeitalter der Restauration." Dissertation, Munster.
In McNamee.

3 HAM, ROSWELL G. "Thomas Otway, Rochester, and Mrs. Barry."
Notes and Queries 149 (5 September):165-67.
Etherege is considered a possible rival to Otway for
Mrs. Barry's affections in the early 1680s.

4 PERRY, HENRY TEN EYCK. The Comic Spirit in Restoration Drama:
Studies in the Comedy of Etherege, Wycherley, Congreve,
Vanbrugh, and Farquhar. New Haven: Yale University Press,
pp. 13-33.
The comic spirit (Meredith's term) steers a course between
satire and sentiment; it highlights the ridiculous for the
intelligent observer. Draws parallels between Sir Frederick
Frollick and Courtal and Dorimant. Sees the love chase as
central to all three plays.

5 THORN-DRURY, G. "Some Notes on Dryden." Review of English
Studies 1 (July):325-26.
From a ms. book compiled by Sir William Howard, Thorn-
Drury cites a variant reading of Dryden's Epilogue to The Man
of Mode.

1926

A BOOKS--NONE

B SHORTER WRITINGS

1 DOBRÉE, BONAMY. A Conversation between Sir George Etherege and
Mr. Fitzjames. London: Hogarth Press, 50 pp.
Set in Ratisbon in 1686, this imaginary conversation
focuses on Rochester, giving personal, literary, and biographical details.

*2 GLADDING, BESSIE A. "The Song in Restoration Drama, 1660-1702."
Dissertation, New York University.
In McNamee.

3 LYNCH, KATHLEEN M. The Social Mode of Restoration Comedy.
University of Michigan Publications in Language and Literature,
no. 3. New York: Macmillan, pp. 137-54, 177-81.
Traces the source of Restoration comedy from Fletcher,
Shirley, and Brome to Etherege, who then imparts it to his
contemporaries Sedley and Shadwell. What Etherege added to
this new kind of play was a reflection of contemporary society.
Despite a heavy emphasis on préciosité, there is a sound

1926

> discussion of all three plays by Etherege. See Ph. D. dissertation, 1924.B4.

4 WAINEWRIGHT, JOHN B. "Sir George Etherege." Notes and Queries 150:126.
> Mentions Scottish Monastery Records reprinted in 1906.B1, and claims Etherege's death date should be 1691.

1927

A BOOKS

1 ETHEREGE, SIR GEORGE. The Dramatic Works. 2 vols. Percy Reprints, no. 6. Edited with introduction and notes by H. F. B. Brett-Smith. Oxford: B. Blackwell, cviii + 325 pp.
> The standard text (although Professor Shirley Strum Kenny is presently at work on the Clarendon edition). Reprinted in 1971.A1. Portions of the introduction reprinted in Loftis, 1966.B13.

B SHORTER WRITINGS

1 BRETT-SMITH, H. F. B. "Review of Bonamy Dobrée's Essays in Biography, 1680-1726." Review of English Studies 3:234-37.
> Corrects some erros in 1925.B1.

2 CAZAMIAN, LOUIS. "Literature of Restoration." In A History of English Literature. 2 vols. By Emile Legoius and Louis Cazamian. Translated by Louis Cazamian and W. D. MacInnes. London: Dent, 2:43-44.
> Etherege's work is quite original though it bears the shade of French influences. Cazamian sees an important progression in each succeeding play; however, "satire [in The Man of Mode] is lost in the merry play of a fastidious irony." Although this history has been revised a number of times up to 1971, the remarks on Etherege remain the same.

3 FOSTER, DOROTHY. "Sir George Etherege: Collections." Notes and Queries 153:417-19, 435-40, 454-59, 472-78.
> Takes up various details of Etherege's life--law cases, birth, apprenticeship, and date of death.

4 HEWINS, ELIZABETH L. "Etherege and Cowley." TLS, 13 October, p. 715.
> Reference in The Man of Mode (III.i.53-56), which Brett-Smith queried, is to Cowley's Davideis (Book III, lines 705-6, in the Waller edition of Cowley).

5 SHADWELL, THOMAS. The Works. 5 vols. Edited by Montague
   Summers. London: Fortune Press, 1:183.
      Remarks by Shadwell on Etherege's She Wou'd if She Cou'd
   in the preface to The Humorists. See 1671.B2.

6 STOLL, ELMER EDGAR. "Literature and Life." In Shakespeare
   Studies: Historical and Comparative in Method. New York:
   Macmillan, pp. 39-89, especially pp. 44-56.
      Takes up Palmer (1913.B3) and Archer (1923.B1) and con-
   cludes that Restoration comedy is art, not life. Enlarged
   discussion from 1924.B5. Reprinted in 1942.B3.

7 WILLIAMSON, GEORGE. "Sir George Etherege and his Guilded
   Butterflies." University of California Chronicle 29 (January):
   44-51.
      A defense of Etherege, going from his life to his comedies.
   Although the comedies are artificial, their world is perfectly
   defined and it is distinctly English. Thus Etherege is a
   "perfect index of his world and what it found amusing"; he
   "epitomized the life of his times in a comedy which became the
   fashion."

                            1928

A BOOKS

1 ETHEREGE, SIR GEORGE. The Letterbook. Edited with introduction
   by Sybil Rosenfeld. Oxford: Oxford University Press. 441 pp.
      Etherege's letters from Ratisbon, 1685-88. From BM Add.
   Ms. 11513. Reprinted in 1971.A2.

2 ETHEREGE, GEORGE. The Man of Mode; or, Sir Fopling Flutter. In
   Readings from British Drama. Edited by Allardyce Nicoll.
   New York: Crowell, pp. 204-7.
      A partial scene from The Man of Mode, III.iii.

B SHORTER WRITINGS

1 ANON. "Sir George Etherege." TLS, 1 March, pp. 138-39.
      Review of Brett-Smith's edition (1927.A1). Suggests that
   because of the paucity of historical evidence, Etherege became
   a legend within twenty years of his death. On the plays:
   "She Wou'd if She Cou'd was the first finished example of
   comedy of manners." Admires Etherege's honesty and truthful-
   ness.

2 ELWIN, MALCOM. "Etherege." In The Playgoer's Handbook to Restoration Drama. London: Jonathan Cape, pp. 60-68.

1928

These introductory remarks on Etherege cite examples of the "rich dialogue." Reprinted in 1966.B9.

3 FOSTER, DOROTHY. "Sir George Etherege: Collections: Addenda." Notes and Queries 154:28.
Adds a revised genealogy of the Etherege family (see 1922. B3), and comments about Sir George's second house on the Saint Jacobus Platz in Ratisbon.

4 _____. "Sir George Etherege." TLS, 31 May, p. 412.
In response to 1928.B1, Foster stresses that much more is known about Etherege than the reviewer makes clear.

5 LACEY, T. A. "'Artificial Comedy.'" TLS, 15 March, p. 188.
Cites yet another example of "real" people of the age being like a plot of a Restoration comedy of manners. See 1928.B9, B10, B11, B12.

6 NETTLETON, GEORGE H. English Drama of the Restoration and Eighteenth Century (1642-1780). New York: Macmillan, pp. 73-77.
Reprint of 1914.B1.

7 NICOLL, ALLARDYCE. A History of Restoration Drama. Cambridge: Cambridge University Press, pp. 234-37, passim.
Reprints of 1923.B3.

8 PINTO, VIVIAN DE SOLA. "Review of The Dramatic Works of Sir George Etherege, edited by H. F. B. Brett-Smith." Review of English Studies 4:341-49.
A review of scholarship on Etherege's works, as well as a commentary on Brett-Smith's edition (1927.A1). See 1929.B1.

9 STOLL, ELMER EDGAR. "'Artificial Comedy.'" TLS, 1 March, p. 150.
From Etherege's Love in a Tub (1664) to Farquhar's Constant Couple (1704) is the period of "artificial comedy"; and while both "literature and life . . . have their traditions, . . . they are not everywhere the same." See 1928.B5, B10, B11, B12.

10 TREVELYAN, G. M. "'Artificial Comedy.'" TLS, 5 January, p. 12.
Makes a parallel of a real eighteenth-century situation with "comedy of manners." Concludes that real people are often as artificial as the comedy of the late Stuart reign. See 1928.B5, B9, B11, B12.

11 _____. "'Artificial Comedy.'" TLS, 8 March, p. 170.
Cites TLS review of Brett-Smith's edition of Etherege

(1927.A1) to show that life is indeed stranger than "comedy of manners." See 1927.B5, B9, B10, B12.

12 WILLIAMS, BASIL. "'Artificial Comedy.'" <u>TLS</u>, 12 January, p. 28.
    Finds Restoration comedy "dull," because it lacks life.
    See 1928.B5, B9, B10, B11.

<u>1929</u>

A BOOKS

1 ETHEREGE, GEORGE. <u>The Man of Mode; or, Sir Fopling Flutter</u>. In <u>British Plays from The Restoration to 1820</u>. Edited with introductions by Montrose J. Moses. Boston: Little, Brown. pp. 119-72.
    Reprinted in 1931.A1.

B SHORTER WRITINGS

1 BRETT-SMITH, H. F. B. "The Works of Etherege." <u>Review of English Studies</u> 5:77-78.
    In answer to Pinto's Review (1928.B8), Brett-Smith announces his plans for a third volume (poems). Also he comments on the use of "square" in <u>Love in a Tub</u> (I.iii.16).

2 CRAWFORD, BARTHOLOW V. "High Comedy in Terms of Restoration Practice." <u>Philological Quarterly</u> 8:339-47.
    Attempts to define high comedy from what happens in various Restoration plays, including <u>The Man of Mode</u>. The best society, intellectually able women, and a heavy emphasis on wit characterize "high comedy."

3 MONTGOMERY, GUY. "The Challenge of Restoration Comedy." In <u>University of California Publications in English</u>. Vol. 1. Berkeley: University of California Press, pp. 135-51.
    The backgroud of Restoration comedy includes a questioning attitude, the new science, changing theology, and an improved status for women. All these changing ideas led to a society that was "in the process of <u>becoming</u> honest," and this process can be seen in the plays. To show how comedy dwindled in the eighteenth century, Montgomery compares Dorimant's opening speech in <u>The Man of Mode</u> with the opening speech of Bevil in <u>The Conscious Lovers</u>. This contrast demonstrates the movement from individual integrity to the confines of law and order. Reprinted in 1966.B13.

4 THORNDIKE, ASHLEY H. <u>English Comedy</u>. New York: Macmillan, pp. 294-98.

1930

Considers <u>Love in a Tub</u> "merely a confusion of heroics,
humours, and intrigues, but praises the dialogue in <u>The Man of
Mode</u>, which "presents a real society and real persons."
Etherege sees the comedy of life through cynicism and wit.

1930

A BOOKS

1 ETHEREGE, GEORGE. <u>The Man of Mode; or, Sir Fopling Flutter</u>. In
Restoration Dramatists. Edited with introductions by F. J.
Tickner. London: T. Nelson, pp. 55-67.
Two scenes: III.iii.123-275 and IV.ii.68-193, with brief
remarks.

B SHORTER WRITINGS

*1 FERGUSON, THOMAS EWING. "The Seventeenth-Century Wit and Fop:
A Study of Restoration Comedy in its Relation to the Life of
Fashion." Dissertation, University of Texas.
Cited in F. M. Litto, <u>American Dissertations on Drama</u>.
Kent: Kent State University Press.

*2 HAYWARD, JOHN, ed. <u>The Letters of Saint-Evremond</u>. London:
Routledge, p. 296.
Notes the relationship between Morin, a well-known dealer
at basset, particularly at the house of the Duchess of Mazarin,
and Etherege. Cited by Thorpe, 1963.A1.

3 HEWINS, ELIZABETH L. "Entertaining in the Grand Manner."
<u>Sewanee Review</u> 38:22-29.
Describes Etherege's celebration in Ratisbon, when the
Prince of Wales was born, "6 July 1689 [sic]." The festivi-
ties began 25 July [1688] and ran for a full three days.
Based on Etherege's own <u>Account</u> (see 1688.A1).

1931

A BOOKS

1 ETHEREGE, GEORGE. <u>The Man of Mode; or, Sir Fopling Flutter</u>. In
<u>British Plays from the Restoration to 1820</u>. Edited with
introductions by Montrose J. Moses. Boston: Little, Brown,
pp. 119-72.
Reprint of 1929.A1.

2 _____. <u>The Man of Mode; or, Sir Fopling Flutter</u>. In <u>Plays of
the Restoration and Eighteenth Century</u>. Edited by Dougald

50

MacMillan and Howard Mumford Jones. New York: Henry Holt,
pp. 82-129. Reprinted in 1938.A1; 1959.A1; 1962.A4; 1964.A1.

3 McCAMIC, FRANCES SMITH [Mrs. Wesley Raynor Taylor, Jr.]. Sir
George Etherege: A Study in Restoration Comedy (1660-1680).
n.p. [NCBEL: Cedar Falls, Iowa, 1931.] 95 pp.
    Deals with Etherege's life, society, and the extent of
French influence on him. Examines each play separately.
Reprinted in 1974.A4.

B SHORTER WRITINGS

1 BOSWELL, ELENORE. "Sir George Etherege." Review of English
Studies 7:207-9.
    Uncovers facts about Etherege's life in PRO records and
chancery reports: the 1657 law suit, sworn in as a gentleman
of the Privy Chamber (31 July 1668), and payment of salary and
expenses while in Ratisbon.

2 PFITZNER, KAETHE. "Die Ausländertypen im Englischen Drama der
Restorationzeit." Dissertation, Breslau, 100 pp.
    Treats Dufoy and Sir Fopling Flutter in her chapter on
the Frenchmen who have come to England.

*3 WILCOX, JOHN. "The Relation of Molière to Restoration Comedy."
Dissertation, University of Michigan.
    See book, 1938.B2.

1932

A BOOKS

1 ETHEREGE, GEORGE. The Man of Mode; or, Sir Fopling Flutter. In
Restoration Plays. Revised edition. Edited by Edmund Gosse.
Everyman's Library. London: Dent; New York: Dutton, pp.
434-509.
    First printed in 1912 without The Man of Mode. Reprinted
in 1962.A5.

B SHORTER WRITINGS

1 FOSTER, DOROTHY. "Sir George Etherege." Review of English
Studies 8:458-59.
    Relates Boswell's findings (1931.B1) to her earlier dis-
coveries (1927.B3; 1928.B3), and shows that Etherege's father
purchased a post at Court--purveyor to the late Queen,
Henrietta Maria.

1932

2 NETTLETON, GEORGE H. English Drama of the Restoration and
Eighteenth Century (1642-1780). New York: Macmillan, pp.
73-77.
    Reprint of 1914.B1.

1933

A BOOKS--NONE

B SHORTER WRITINGS

1 ELLEHAUGE, MARTIN. English Restoration Drama: Its Relation to
Past English and Past and Contemporary French Drama. From
Jonson via Molière to Congreve. Copenhagen: Levin and
Munksgaard, passim.
    After showing how Restoration drama evolved from Elizabe-
than and French sources, Ellehauge then considers action,
character, dialogue, and spirit. Promises more than it
delivers. Badly proofread. Reprinted 1974.B2.

1934

A BOOKS

*1 ETHEREGE, GEORGE. The Man of Mode; or, Sir Fopling Flutter. In
Representative English Drama from Dryden to Sheridan. Edited
by Frederick Tupper and James W. Tupper. New York: Oxford
University Press, pp. 124-66.

B SHORTER WRITINGS

*1 FUJII, AKIO. "Sir George Etherege." Studies in English Litera-
ture (Tokyo) 14:155-81.
    Article in Japanese; listed MHRA Annual Bibliography.

*2 JANSEN, HILDE. "Soziologische Selbst-Charakteristik der Adels
in der Restaurations Komedie." Dissertation, University of
Bonn.
    In McNamee.

*3 MacLEOD, WILLIAM R. "Stage Repertoires of the First Decade of
the Restoration." Dissertation, Fordham University.
    In McNamee.

4 NOYES, ROBERT G. "Contemporary Musical Settings of the Songs
in Restoration Drama." English Literary History 1:325-44.
    Songs from the plays that circulated in contemporary music
books till 1700, includes several lyrics by Etherege. See

1936.B2.

5 ROSENFELD, SYBIL. "Sir George Etherege in Ratisbon." Review of
English Studies 10:177-89.
Holograph letters in the Middleton papers at the BM (Add.
Ms. 41836 and 41837) include 134 not published in the Letterbook (1928.A1). Rosenfeld concentrates on quoting from letters
that tell about Etherege the envoy, his life and his activity
in Ratisbon.

6 STOLL, ELMER EDGAR. "The Beau Monde at the Restoration." Modern
Language Notes 49:425-32.
In Restoration drama, the audience learns to distinguish
the true beau monde from the false. Cites parallel passages
from Beaumont and Fletcher and from Etherege to show the dif-
ference and the continuity between Jacobean and Restoration
drama.

7 SUMMERS, MONTAGUE. A Bibliography of the Restoration Drama.
London: Fortune Press, [1934 or 1935].
Provides first performance dates, first and subsequent
editions printed in Etherege's lifetime, and important reprints up to 1927.

8 _____. The Restoration Theatre. London: Kegan Paul; New York:
Macmillan, passim.
Uses quotations from Restoration plays by Etherege and
others to comment about the physical theatres and the conditions of performance. Appendix A: R. Gould's "The Playhouse,
a Satyr." See 1709.B1.

9 THORPE, WILLARD, ed. Songs from Restoration Theater. Princeton:
Princeton University Press.
Reprints Etherege's songs in plays by Southerne (1684.B1)
and Tate (1685.B1).

1935

A BOOKS

1 ETHEREGE, GEORGE. The Man of Mode; or, Sir Fopling Flutter. In
English Plays, 1660-1820. Edited by A. E. Morgan. New York:
Harper, pp. 109-168.

B SHORTER WRITINGS

1 CROISSANT, DEWITT C. "Early Sentimental Comedy." In Essays in
Dramatic Literature: The Parrott Presentation Volume. Edited

1935

by Hardin Craig. Princeton: Princeton University Press.
pp. 47-71.
Considers sentimental comedy "a debased romanticism" and
discusses plays of the Restoration with these characteristics,
including Love in a Tub (Graciana labeled a self-sacrificing
maiden) and The Man of Mode (Bellinda's reform is sentimental).
Strains to make his case.

*2 JOHNSON, FRANK L. "The Conventions of Restoration Comedy."
Dissertation, University of Wisconsin.
In McNamee.

3 SUMMERS, MONTAGUE. The Playhouse of Pepys. London: Kegan Paul,
pp. 307-13.
Collects information from Downes (1708.B1), provides comments on plots, gives later cast lists, and concludes his
discussion by calling The Man of Mode "the most immoral comedy
I know."

1936

A BOOKS--NONE

B SHORTER WRITINGS

1 HARBAGE, ALFRED. Cavalier Drama. New York: Modern Language
Association, pp. 86-88.
From the reign of Charles I to the death of Davenant,
Harbage finds a number of strands, especially plays by courtiers
for the court. About Love in a Tub, he points out the com-
mingling of old farce and old tragicomedy. Nevertheless, the
play is novel owing to Etherege's skill and spirit.

2 NOYES, ROBERT G. "Songs from Restoration Drama in Contemporary
and Eighteenth-Century Poetical Miscellanies." English
Literary History 3:291-316.
Lists a number of songs that found their way into poetical
miscellanies. The number of reprintings gives an idea of the
popularity. Includes a large number of Etherege's songs.
See 1934.B4.

3 PERKINSON, RICHARD H. "Topographical Comedy in the Seventeenth
Century." English Literary History 3:270-290.
The mention of real locations in Jacobean and Restoration
comedies gives the dramas plausibility and probability. Cites
such usage by Etherege. Plays should not be a transcript of
real life, nor simply be social documents, but a known locale
aids the plot or theme of a playwright.

1937

A BOOKS--NONE

B SHORTER WRITINGS

1 KNIGHTS, L. C. "Restoration Comedy: The Reality and the Myth."
   Scrutiny 6:122-43.
        This famous attack against Restoration comedy concludes
   that the genre is "trivial, gross, and dull." Specifically
   on The Man of Mode, he remarks "the 'real values' simply are
   not there." This essay has forced later commentators to
   defend the plays on aesthetic rather than moral grounds.
   Reprinted in 1946.B2; 1966.B11; 1973.A2.

2 NOYES, ROBERT GALE, and LAMSON, ROY, JR. "Broadside-Ballad
   Versions of the Songs in Restoration Drama." Harvard Studies
   in Philology and Literature 19:199-218.
        Songs from plays are often expanded into broadsides, and
   sometimes altered. Mentions two examples from Etherege.

1938

A BOOKS

1 ETHEREGE, GEORGE. The Man of Mode; or, Sir Fopling Flutter. In
   Plays of the Restoration and Eighteenth Century. Edited by
   Dougald MacMillan and Howard Mumford Jones. New York: Henry
   Holt, pp. 82-129.
        Reprint of 1931.A2, with additions.

B SHORTER WRITINGS

1 DOBRÉE, BONAMY. "Etherege." In Restoration Comedy, 1660-1720.
   London: Oxford University Press, pp. 58-77.
        Reprint of 1924.B2.

2 WILCOX, JOHN. "Etherege." The Relation of Molière to Restoration
   Comedy. New York: Columbia University Press, pp. 70-81.
        Sets out to correct Gosse's inaccuracies (1881.B2). Dis-
   misses earlier views that Etherege borrowed from Molière.
   See Ph.D. dissertation, 1931.B3; reprinted in 1964.B8.

1939

A BOOKS

1 ETHEREGE, GEORGE. The Man of Mode; or, Sir Fopling Flutter. In

1939

    <u>British Dramatists from Dryden to Sheridan</u>. Edited by George
H. Nettleton and Arthur E. Case. Boston: Houghton-Mifflin,
pp. 153-95.
        Reprinted in 1969.A1, with revised headnotes and bibliog-
raphy.

B SHORTER WRITINGS

1 DENNIS, JOHN. <u>Critical Works</u>. 2 vols. Edited by E. N. Hooker.
    Baltimore: Johns Hopkins University Press, 1939-43, passim.
    Numerous references to Etherege. See 1702.B1; 1722.B1.

2 WILSON, JOHN HAROLD. "Two Poems Ascribed to Rochester." <u>Modern
Language Notes</u> 54:458-60.
        Ascribes the song "Since Death on all lays his impartial
hand" to Etherege, rather than to Rochester.

1940

A BOOKS--NONE

B SHORTER WRITINGS

*1 BIGELOW, LESLIE PLATT. "The Style and the Wit of Restoration
    Comedy of Manners." Dissertation, Ohio State University.
        In McNamee.

2 GASSNER, JOHN. "From Etherege to Sheridan." In <u>Masters of the
Drama</u>. New York: Random House, pp. 304-14.
        Brief remarks on each of the plays. Sees Harriet as "an
unconventional heroine." Reprinted in 1945.B2; 1954.B3.

3 HUGHES, LEO. "Attitudes of Some Restoration Dramatists Toward
    Farce." <u>Philological Quarterly</u> 19:268-87.
        Notes Dryden's continuing attack on farce in his epilogue
to <u>The Man of Mode</u>.

4 NICOLL, ALLARDYCE. <u>A History of Restoration Drama</u>. Cambridge:
    Cambridge University Press, pp. 234-7, passim.
        Reprint of 1923.B3.

5 PAINE, CLARENCE. "The Comedy of Manners (1660-1700): A
    Reference Guide to the Comedy of the Restoration." <u>Bulletin
of Bibliography and Dramatic Index</u> 17 (1940-42):70-72, 97-99,
116-17, 145-48.
        Lists twelve entries for Etherege (all included in this
bibliography) in this brief guide published over a two-year
period.

1941

A BOOKS--NONE

B SHORTER WRITINGS

1 SAVILE, HENRY. "Letter to the Earl of Rochester." In The
    Rochester-Savile Letters, 1671-1680. Edited by John Harold
    Wilson. Columbus: Ohio State University Press.
        Reprint of 1907.B3, with annotations.

1942

A BOOKS--NONE

B SHORTER WRITINGS

*1 ALLEMAN, GELLERT SPENCER. "English Law and the Materials of
    Restoration Comedy." Dissertation, University of Pennsylvania.
        In McNamee. See book, 1942.B2.

2 _____. Matrimonial Law and the Materials of Restoration Comedy.
    Wallingford, Pa.: n.p., passim.
        Analyzes the way Restoration comedy uses existing marriage
    laws. Treats marriage contracts, irregular marriages, and
    termination of marriages. See Ph.D. dissertation, 1942.B1.

3 STOLL, ELMER EDGAR. "Literature and Life." In Shakespeare
    Studies: Historical and Comparative in Method. New York:
    Macmillan, pp. 39-89, especially pp. 44-56.
        Reprint of 1927.B6.

1943

A BOOKS--NONE

B SHORTER WRITINGS

1 HOUGHTON, WALTER E., JR. "Lamb's Criticism of Restoration
    Comedy." English Literary History 10:61-72.
        Demonstrates that Lamb's theory of Restoration comedy
    (1822.B1) is "a highly sensitive interpretation."

*2 MIGNON, ELIZABETH. "Old Men and Women in Restoration Comedy of
    Manners." Dissertation, Bryn Mawr.
        In McNamee. See book, 1947.B2.

Writings by and about Etherege

1944

A BOOKS--NONE

B SHORTER WRITINGS

1 PELTZ, CATHARINE WALSH. "The Neo-classic Lyric, 1660-1725."
   English Literary History 11:92-116.
   Classifies types of lyrics by 19 poets writing between
   1660-1725. Poems of Etherege discussed on pp. 100 & 109-10.

1945

A BOOKS--NONE

B SHORTER WRITINGS

1 BENTLEY, ERIC RUSSELL. "The Views of Mr. Symons." Kenyon Review
   7:477-80.
   Rejoinder to Symons; see 1945.B5.

2 GASSNER, JOHN. "From Etherege to Sheridan." In Masters of the
   Drama. New York: Random House, pp. 304-14.
   Reprint of 1940.B2.

3 HOWARTH, R. G. "Untraced Quotations in Etherege." Notes and
   Queries 188 (June):281.
   Identifies the source of Dorimant's quotation in The Man
   of Mode (II.ii.170-71), as being from The Phoenix Nest, a
   poem ascribed to Matthew Raydon. The proverb on "ale and
   history" has an analogue in Bishop Corbet's "Iter Boreale."

*4 SCOTT, VIRGIL J. "Topical Non-conformist Satire in Restoration
   Comedy, 1660-1685." Dissertation, Ohio State University,
   336 pp.
   In McNamee.

5 SYMONS, JULIAN. "Restoration Comedy (Reconsiderations II)."
   Kenyon Review 7:185-97.
   Mentions Etherege as he tries to show a moral continuum
   from the Restoration through Sheridan to Wilde, Pinero, and
   Shaw. See rejoinder, 1945.B1.

1946

A BOOKS

1 ETHEREGE, GEORGE. The Man of Mode; or, Sir Fopling Flutter. In

1947

Chief Patterns of World Drama. Edited, with an introduction
by W. S. Clark, II. Boston: Houghton-Mifflin, pp. 534-92.

B SHORTER WRITINGS

1 DOBRÉE, BONAMY. "Etherege." In Restoration Comedy, 1660-1720.
    London: Oxford University Press, pp. 58-77.
        Reprint of 1924.B2.

2 KNIGHTS, L.C. "Restoration Comedy: The Reality and the Myth."
    In Explorations: Essays in Criticism Mainly on the Literature
    of the Seventeenth Century. London: Chatto and Windus; New
    York: George W. Stewart, 1947.
        Reprint of 1937.B1.

3 MANDACH, ANDRÉ de. Molière et la Comédie de Moeurs en Angleterre
    (1660-68). In Essai de Litterature Comparée. Neuchatel,
    Switzerland: Baconnière, passim.
        Suggests that Tartuffe probably inspired She Wou'd if She
    Cou'd, and that Lady Cockwood is "un Tartuffe feminin."

*4 SMITH, JOHN HARRINGTON. "Heroes and Heroines in English Comedy,
    1660-1750." Dissertation, Harvard University.
        In McNamee. See book, 1948.B3.

1947

A BOOKS--NONE

B SHORTER WRITINGS

*1 CLANCY, JAMES HARVEY. "The Humorists: An Elizabethan Method of
    Characterization as Modified by Etherege and Congreve."
    Dissertation, Stanford University.
        In McNamee.

2 MIGNON, ELIZABETH. "Etherege." In Crabbed Age and Youth: the
    Old Men and Women in Restoration Comedy of Manners. Durham,
    N. C.: Duke University Press, pp. 36-47.
        Lady Cockwood is clearly too old for the youthful game
    she tries to play in She Wou'd if She Cou'd, and she thus
    becomes a foil for Ariana and Gatty, the "young" ladies. In
    The Man of Mode, Old Bellair and Lady Woodvil, the elders,
    have outlived their generation. Etherege sets the tone for
    the comedies of the next forty years with his treatment of
    old men and women as representatives of outdated morals and
    rigid attitudes.

1947

3 WILSON, JOHN HAROLD. "Etherege's <u>Julia</u>." <u>Modern Language Notes</u>
62:40-42.
Etherege's mistress in 1686-87, an actress from Nurenberg,
is not named Julia, the allusion is literary, referring to
Ovid in his banishment. See the letter to Cooke in Bracher,
1974.A1, pp. 163-64.

1948

A BOOKS--NONE

B SHORTER WRITINGS

1 BELJAME, ALEXANDRE. <u>Men of letters and the English Public in the</u>
<u>Eighteenth Century, 1660-1744</u>. Translated by Emily O. Lormier.
Edited by Bonamy Dobrée. London: Kegan Paul.
Translation of 1881.B1.

2 SHERBURN, GEORGE. "Restoration and Eighteenth Century." In
<u>A Literary History of England</u>. Edited by A. C. Baugh. New
York: Appleton-Century-Crofts, pp. 763-66.
"Restoration comedy is rather less a representation of
life than it is a commentary on manners." Sees two "movements"
in Restoration comedy: 1668-76 and 1693-1707. Notes the four
plots in <u>Love in a Tub</u> and the clever detached dialogue in
<u>She Wou'd if She Cou'd</u>. <u>The Man of Mode</u> has a succession of
episodic scenes, "delightfully comic and skillfully written."

3 SMITH, JOHN HARRINGTON. <u>The Gay Couple in Restoration Comedy</u>.
Cambridge, Mass.: Harvard University Press, pp. 51-92.
Divides Restoration comedy into three periods on the basis
of the "gay couple": gay comedy, 1660-75; cynical comedy,
1675-87; and exemplary comedy, 1687-1707 (excluding sentimental
comedy). Etherege's first two plays are gay comedies, in
which nobody gets hurt, whereas in <u>The Man of Mode</u> the gallant
becomes more intellectual and cynical. While Harriet is a
match for Dorimant, the ably witty female rarely gets repeated
in these middle comedies, which stress sexual games. Reprinted
in 1971.B9.

4 WILSON, JOHN HAROLD. <u>The Court Wits of the Restoration</u>.
Princeton: Princeton University Press, 264 pp., passim.
The lives and literature of the courtiers of Charles II,
told with verve. Wilson describes <u>Love in a Tub</u> as a "madcap
comedy," where farcical episodes are set alongside a serious
love/honor plot; <u>She Wou'd if She Cou'd</u> is in the tradition of
Caroline comedy; and <u>The Man of Mode</u> exhibits an elegant prose
style. Reprinted in 1967.B9.

1949

A BOOKS--NONE

B SHORTER WRITINGS

1 KRUTCH, JOSEPH WOOD. <u>Comedy and Conscience after the Restoration</u>.
  New York: Columbia University Press, pp. 18-19, 174-76,
  passim.
      Reprint of 1924.B3, with index and updated bibliography
  by G. S. Alleman.

2 NICHOL, J. W. "Dame Mary Etherege." <u>Modern Language Notes</u>
  69:419-22.
      Etherege's wife, the widow of Edmund Arnold, was born
  Mary Sheppard, daughter of John Sheppard of London, and married
  Arnold before 1648. Arnold's legal career continued until his
  death in 1676. Thus Mary would have been 45 to 50 when she
  married Etherege several years after Arnold's death. The
  exact date of the marriage is not known.

3 SHERBO, ARTHUR. "A Note on <u>The Man of Mode</u>." <u>Modern Language
  Notes</u> 64:343-44.
      Points out previously unnoticed parallels between <u>The Man
  of Mode</u> and Molière's <u>Les Précieuses Ridicules</u>, when Sir
  Fopling calls for his equipage (<u>The Man of Mode</u>, III.iii).

4 _____. "Sir Fopling Flutter and Beau Hewitt." <u>Notes and Queries</u>
  194:296-303.
      Contemporary documents on the life of Sir George [Beau]
  Hewitt show that Oldys's information (from the actor John
  Bowman) in <u>Biographia Britannica</u> (1750.B2) is incorrect.
  Hewitt is not the model for Sir Fopling Flutter. See 1973.B4.

1950

A BOOKS--NONE

B SHORTER WRITINGS

*1 FREEHAFER, JOHN H. "The Emergence of Sentimental Comedy, 1660-
   1707." Dissertation, University of Pennsylvania.
      Cited in <u>Doctoral Dissertations Accepted by American
   Universities, 1949-50</u>, no. 17. New York: H. W. Wilson, 1950,
   p. 201.

2 FUJIMURA, THOMAS H. "The Comedy of Wit, 1660-1710." Dissertation, Columbia University, 314 pp.

1950

"Writers of the period were more concerned with <u>wit</u> than
with <u>manners</u>." Catalogues types of wit. Etherege's comic
world is characterized by elegance, intellectual distinction,
and the graceful and sensible acceptance of life. See book,
1952.B1.

3 GAGEN, JEAN ELISABETH. "Foreshadowings of tbe New Woman in the
English Drama of the Seventeenth and early Eighteenth Century."
Dissertation, Columbia University, 311 pp.
The "New Woman" achieved social, intellectual and spiritu-
al equality with men. Various types are catalogued. See book,
1954.B2.

4 LOFTIS, JOHN. "The Genesis of Steele's 'The Conscious Lovers.'"
In <u>Essays Critical and Historical Dedicated to Lily B. Campbell</u>.
Berkeley: University of California Press, pp. 173-82.
Steele's idea for <u>The Conscious Lovers</u> may have come as
early as 1710-11, when his work on the <u>Spectator</u> may have
helped him sharpen his plan for the play and the characters,
especially Bevil, Jr., who derives from the ideas he used in
attacking Dorimant of <u>The Man of Mode</u>. See 1711.B3, B4, B5.

1951

A BOOKS--NONE

B SHORTER WRITINGS

1 BATESON, F. W. "Contributions to a Dictionary of Critical Terms:
I. Comedy of Manners." <u>Essays in Criticism</u> 1:89-93.
Both Addison and Steele used "genteel comedy," but the
term coined by Lamb was "comedy of manners." (1922.B1) Later
in the nineteenth century, Stopford Brooke (1876.B2) applied
the term to Behn, Etherege, and Wycherley. But the term was
probably made current by George Meredith before being used as
a book title by John Palmer (1913.B3).

2 DOBRÉE, BONAMY. "Etherege." In <u>Restoration Comedy, 1660-1720</u>.
London: Oxford University Press, pp. 58-77.
Reprint of 1924.B2.

3 FELTHAM, FREDRIK G. "The Quality of the Wit in Comedies of
Etherege, Wycherley, Congreve, and Shadwell." Dissertation,
University of Chicago, 212 pp.
Chapter 2 (pp. 25-59) points out that wit is the finished
part of a gentleman. <u>Love in a Tub</u> is too cluttered by farce
to reveal effective verbal wit. <u>She Wou'd if She Cou'd</u> is a
closed world of "wits and bawds and fools," yet the wit is

dramatically functional. In The Man of Mode, "wit is
Dorimant's highest achievement, his chiefest grace." Nevertheless, Harriet "out-wits" him: "through wit one achieves
an ironic remove and thereby preserves himself [or herself]
in freedom."

4 LEECH, CLIFFORD. "Restoration Comedy: The Earlier Phase."
    Essays in Criticism 1:165-84.
        Although Leech begins by classifying comedies as 1) man-
    ners, and 2) humours, he finds that these categories are
    artificial because a unity of effect was rarely achieved.
    Cites Etherege's plays to show a progression in structure,
    dialogue, and thought.

                              1952

A BOOKS

*1 UNDERWOOD, DALE. "The Comic Art of Etherege." Dissertation,
    Yale University.
        In McNamee. See book, 1957.A1.

B SHORTER WRITINGS

1 FUJIMURA, THOMAS H. The Restoration Comedy of Wit. Princeton:
    Princeton University Press, 232 pp., passim.
        Sets wit against its intellectual background in the age,
    then applies the idea of wit to the comedies of Etherege,
    Wycherley, and Congreve. In Chapter 5, Etherege himself is
    established as a "true wit" and a discussion of the plays fol-
    lows: Sir Frederick, in Love in a Tub, lacks a sense of
    decorum and will not qualify as a "true wit." Lady Cockwood's
    flaw, in She Wou'd if She Cou'd, is her pretension to conven-
    tional morality. Wit, in The Man of Mode, arises from natural-
    istic impulses: "Dorimant [is] characterized by malice and
    judgment, Medley by fanciful and skeptical wit, and Harriet
    by natural spontaneous wit." Reprinted in 1968.B6. Section
    on The Man of Mode reprinted in 1973.A2.

2 HISCOCK, W. G. "John Evelyn, Jun., as a Literary Critic." TLS,
    27 June, p. 421.
        Included in reading by the diarist's son in 1696 is this
    remark about Love in a Tub: "Very good, all but the love and
    honour part in Rhime, which would make a dog vomit."

3 KRONENBERGER, LOUIS. The Thread of Laughter: Chapters on the
    English Stage from Jonson to Maugham. New York: Knopf, pp.
    44-53.

1952

> Sees the Widow Rich-Sir Frederick plot as "something new in English comedy." She Wou'd if She Cou'd has a "quality of airiness," chiefly provided by the young lovers. The Man of Mode "mingles brutality with lightness," and carries a "faintly elegaic apprehension."

4 NICOLL, ALLARDYCE. A History of Restoration Drama. Cambridge: Cambridge University Press, pp. 234-37, passim
> Slightly revised printing of 1923.B3.

5 ROSENFELD, SYBIL. "The Second Letterbook of Sir George Etherege." Review of English Studies, n.s. 3:19-27.
> Harvard letterbooks at the Houghton Library (fMS Thr. 11 and fMS Thr. 11.1) contains over ninety letters of Etherege, covering the last ten months of his envoyship, plus a list of twenty-nine letters between 20 February and 28 September 1689.

1953

A BOOKS

1 ETHEREGE, GEORGE. The Man of Mode; or, Sir Fopling Flutter. In Cavalcade of Comedy. Edited by Louis Kronenberger. New York: Simon and Schuster, pp. 82-116.

2 _____. The Man of Mode; or, Sir Fopling Flutter. In Restoration Plays. With an introduction by Brice Harris. New York: Random House/Modern Library, pp. vii-xviii, 155-243.
> Harris notes in his introduction that Dorimant "shared his typical qualities with many of the courtiers of Charles II." Reprinted in 1955.A1, 1966.A2.

B SHORTER WRITINGS

1 GOODMAN, OSCAR BERNARD. "English New Comedy." Dissertation, Columbia University, 284 pp.
> Argues that Restoration comedy is in the tradition of Greek new comedy: "In Menander and in Etherege there is . . . urbanity, refinement, consciousness of style and structure, and above all, a humanistic air . . . ." DA, 14 (1954):110-11.

*2 SINGH, S. "A Study of the Critical Theory of the Restoration Drama as Expressed in the Dedications, Prefaces, Prologues, Epilogues, and other Dramatic Criticism of the Period." Dissertation, University of London.
> In McNamee.

1954

3 WEISS, SAMUEL ABBA. "Hobbism and Restoration Comedy." Dissertation, Columbia University, 240 pp.
Treats Hobbesian doctrine as it appears in Restoration
comedy from Dryden through Steele. <u>DA</u>, 13 (1953):114.

1954

A BOOKS--NONE

B SHORTER WRITINGS

*1 FEDDERN, GERT-DETLEF. "Der Parallelismus als Heimsches Stilele-
ment in der Prosadiktion und Komposition der Englischen
Restaurationskomödie." Dissertation, Berlin (Frei).
In McNamee.

2 GAGEN, JEAN ELISABETH. <u>The New Woman: Her Emergence in English
Drama, 1600-1730</u>. New York: Twayne, passim.
Catalogues types of women in drama and their changing
status. Brief mention to Ariana and Gatty (<u>She Wou'd if She
Cou'd</u>) and Harriet (<u>The Man of Mode</u>) in her chapter titled
"Ladies in Command." See Ph.D. Dissertation, 1950.B3.

3 GASSNER, JOHN. "From Etherege to Sheridan." In <u>Masters of the
Drama</u>. New York: Dover, pp. 304-14.
Reprint of 1940.B2.

*4 HOWLING, ROBERT T. "Moral Aspects of Restoration Comedy." Dis-
sertation, Pennsylvania State University, 199 pp.
Cited in <u>Abstracts of Doctoral Dissertations</u>, 17 (1955):
479.

5 McDOWELL, MARGARET BLAINE. "Moral Purpose in Restoration Comedy."
Dissertation, University of Iowa, 438 pp.
Examines 150 plays between 1660-1700 for moral aspects,
then concentrates on six plays, including The Man of Mode, to
show how a "serious satiric scrutiny underlies the basic
design of plot, characterization, and dialogue." <u>DA</u>, 14
(1954), 1710-11.

6 NEVILLE, MARIE. "Etherege and Holbein." <u>Notes and Queries</u> 199:
157.
Notes Etherege's poetic reference, in the <u>Letterbook</u> (1928.
A1, pp. 80-82), to Holbein's portrait of Henry VIII and Jane
Seymour, probably the one destroyed in a fire of 1698.

7 PINTO, V. de S. <u>Restoration Carnival</u>. London: Folio Society,
pp. 71-107.

1955

        Biographical sketch with a discussion of the plays, mostly
plot summary. Also prints (pp. 91-107) a number of the poems.

<u>1955</u>

A BOOKS

1 ETHEREGE, GEORGE. <u>The Man of Mode; or, Sir Fopling Flutter</u>. In
  <u>Restoration Plays</u>. With an introduction by Brice Harris.
  New York: Random House/Modern Library, pp. vii-xviii, 153-
  243.
      Reprint of 1953.A2.

B SHORTER WRITINGS

1 BARNHART, WILLIAM J. "High Comedy and Low Comedy in England,
  1660-1676; A Study in the Development of the Comedy of Manners." Dissertation, University of North California.
      In McNamee.

2 BERKELEY, DAVID S. "Préciosité and the Restoration Comedy of
  Manners." <u>Huntington Library Quarterly</u> 18:109-28.
      Understanding préciosité allows audiences of Restoration
  comedies to discern the false wit from the true one, to tell
  real love from feigned love, and to differentiate the whining
  lover from the true gallant. Examples from all of Etherege's
  plays show how he used the convention of préciosité.

3 _____. "Some Notes on Probability in Restoration Drama." <u>Notes
  and Queries</u> 200:237-39, 342-43.
      Although Restoration writers adapted the Elizabethan
  couplet, it does not increase the believeability of the
  characters. Shows how the couplets in the high plot of <u>Love
  in a Tub</u> are played off against the prose of Dufoy.

4 DOBRÉE, BONAMY. "Etherege." In <u>Restoration Comedy: 1660-1720</u>.
  London: Oxford University Press, pp. 58-77.
      Reprint of 1924.B2.

5 EVELYN, JOHN. <u>The Diary</u>. 6 vols. Edited by E. S. de Beer.
  Oxford: Clarendon Press, 3:371.
      Reprint of 1664.B1.

6 MUDRICK, MARVIN. "Restoration Comedy and Later." In <u>English
  Stage Comedy</u> (English Institute Essays, 1954). Edited by W.
  K. Wimsatt, Jr. New York: Columbia University Press, pp.
  98-125.
      An important answer to Knights (1937.B1); demonstrates
  that "the comedy of manners does not necessarily trifle; it is

hospitable to serious issues." Some remarks on Etherege, though The Country Wife and The Way of the World get the majority of the discussion.

7 VAN DER WEELE, STEVEN JOHN. "The Critical Reputation of Restoration Comedy in Modern Times." Dissertation, University of Wisconsin, 771 pp.
    A review of criticism, concentrating on the twentieth century. Etherege emerges as "the innovator of manners comedy." DA, 16 (1956):344. See book, 1978.B6.

1956

A BOOKS--NONE

B SHORTER WRITINGS

1 CECIL, C. D. "Restoration Comic Diction: Modes of Speech in Etherege, Wycherley, and Congreve." Dissertation, Oxford University.
    Studies diction in Etherege, Wycherley, and Congreve. Wit for Etherege and Wycherley is arrogance, combined with frequent indiference to others. A study of the language of fools, polite society, and the vulgar demonstrates how "speech manners" render a clear verbal class distinction.

*2 DALLDORFF, HORST. "Die Welt der Restaurationskomödie. Ein Querschnitt druch die Lustspiele Hauptsächlich von Etherege, Wycherley, und Congreve zur Erfassung ihrer Stofflichen Wesenszüge." Dissertation, Kiel, xiii + 300 pp.
    In McNamee.

3 FUJIMURA, THOMAS H. "Etherege at Constantinople." PMLA 71:465-71.
    Biographical information about Etherege's years in Turkey, 1668-71, showing the breadth of his knowledge of the world as well as the stage.

*4 HOLLAND, NORMAN NORWOOD, JR. "A Critical Reading of the Comedies of Etherege, Wycherley, and Congreve." Dissertation, Harvard University.
    In McNamee; see book, 1959.B3.

5 KORNBLUTH, MARTIN LEONARD. "Frienship in Fashion: The Dramatic Treatment of Friendship in the Restoration and Eighteenth Century." Dissertation, Pennsyvalnia State University, 234 pp.
    Surveys 83 plays between 1664-1777, and finds that friendship usually reigns over all other emotions--love, honor,

1956

> loyalty--but occasionally it becomes "a means to some other
> end, usually lust." DA 17 (1957):361.

6 RYMER, THOMAS. "A Short View of Tragedy." In Critical Works.
  Edited by Curt A. Zimansky. New Haven: Yale University Press.
  p. 160.
     Othello's remarks to Desdemona in Act 5 sound like "the
  Very Soul and Quintessence of Sir George Etheridge." See
  1693.B1.

7 URE, PETER. "The Widow of Ephesus: Some Reflections on an
  International Comic Theme." Durham Univ. Journal 49 [n.s. 18]:
  1-9.
     Notes Etherege's change of the ancient story about the
  widow (Letterbook--1928.A1--pp. 416-21; Letters--1974.A1--pp.
  92-7), included in a letter to the Duke of Buckingham. See
  also 1762.A1.

8 WAIN, JOHN. "Restoration Comedy and its Modern Critics." Essays
  in Criticism 6:367-85.
     Incomplete essay on Restoration comedy as good documents
  to study the period, but bad plays. Wain, however, makes an
  exception with Etherege's The Man of Mode because it carries
  "the courage of its author's convictions." See 1957.B7 for
  the complete essay.

1957

A BOOKS

1 UNDERWOOD, DALE. Etherege and Seventeenth-Century Comedy of
  Manners. Yale Studies in English, no. 135. New Haven: Yale
  University Press, 165 pp.
     Using Etherege's plays to consider the genre of Restora-
  tion comedy, Underwood deals with the two traditions of the
  protagonists: 1) the honnête homme (derived from the heroic
  tradition and Christian humanism), and 2) the libertine (derived from Machiavellian and Hobbesian concepts). Deals also
  with background, language, and connections with Elizabethan
  and Jacobean drama (realistic elements). Ultimately finds
  the plays of Etherege and most Restoration dramatists more
  complex than they have been seen heretofore. See Ph.D.,
  Dissertation, 1952.A1. Chapter 5 reprinted in 1966.B13.
  Chapter 6 reprinted in 1966.B14.

B SHORTER WRITINGS

1 BARBER, C. L. The Idea of Honour in the English Drama, 1591-1700.

Gothenburg Studies in English, no. 6. Göteborg: Elanders
Boktryckeri Aktiebolag, 362 pp.
    Statistical study of the term "honour." Barber notes the
frequent use of "honour" in She Wou'd if She Cou'd, 53 times,
and more than in any other play written from 1661-70. More
than half of the usages are by Lady Cockwood.

2 BATESON, F. W. "Second Thoughts: II. L. C. Knights and Resto-
    ration Comedy." Essays in Criticism 7:56-67.
        Undertakes a defense of Restoration comedy on the basis of
    its "implicit seriousness." Speaks up for Congreve and
    Wycherley, as Wain (1956.B8) had for Etherege. Shows that
    other approaches than Knights' (1937.B1) are possible. Re-
    printed in 1966.B13; 1972.B1.

3 COLLINS, P. A. W. "Restoration Comedy." In From Dryden to
    Johnson. Vol. 4 of Pelican Guide to English Literature.
    Edited by Boris Ford. Harmondsworth, Middlesex; Baltimore:
    Penguin, pp. 156-72.
        Some attention to The Man of Mode, but concludes that
    Etherege's "vision remains peripheral. Etherege in general
    suffers (actually or by modish affection) from emotional
    constipation."

4 EMPSON, WILLIAM, and HOLLAND, NORMAN N. "The Critical Forum:
    Restoration Comedy Again." Essays in Criticism 7:318-22.
        Two responses to articles by Wain (1956.B8) and Bateson
    (1957.B2): Empson defends Congreve's Mirabell, and Holland
    sides with Bateson against Wain's sociological and Knights's
    anti-aesthetic readings. Holland's remarks on The Man of Mode
    here, are expanded in his 1959.B3 book.

*5 MINOR, CHARLES B. "An Analytical Study of Grammatical Uses and
    Tendencies in Some Restoration Playwrights of Comedies with
    Comparisons to the Present-Day Usages and Tendencies." Dis-
    sertation, University of Denver.
        In McNamee.

6 OHARA, DAVID M. "The Restoration Comic Perspective: A Study of
    the Comedy of Manners." Dissertation, University of Pennsyl-
    vania, 237 pp.
        In surveying comedies from 1663-1707, sees the basic plot
    of the comedy of manners as a "love-game." Finds The Man of
    Mode "realistic," except "in only one fantastic person of
    monumental affectation--the unsurpassed Sir Fopling Flutter."
    DA, 17 (1957):3021-22.

1957

7 WAIN, JOHN. "Restoration Comedy and its Modern Critics." In
   Preliminary Essays. London: Macmillan, pp. 1-35.
      Sees Etherege making a serious social comment on the ethos
   of the age. Despite the ruthlessness of some of the characters,
   their dialogue "has at least the harsh ring of truth."
   Finished essay of the incomplete 1956.B8. See Vernon's remarks, 1962.B8, on Wain's overlooking of conventions.

1958

A BOOKS--NONE

B SHORTER WRITINGS

1 BURTON, K. M. P. Restoration Literature. London: Hutchinson
   University Library, pp. 74-79.
      Following the praise of Wain (1956.B8 and 1957.B7), Burton
   speaks well of The Man of Mode, but much of what is said is
   plot summary glued together with quotable quotations from the
   play.

2 CORDER, JIMMIE WAYNE. "The Restoration Way of the World: A
   Study of Restoration Comedy." Dissertation, University of
   Oklahoma, 359 pp.
      Believes the comedies of Etherege, Wycherley, and Congreve
   to be better than those of Shadwell, Vanbrugh, Farquhar, Cibber,
   and Steele because the former show an "epistemological progres-
   sion in which the hero . . . is educated in ways of decorum,"
   whereas the latter "rely too much on action." DA, 19 (1959):
   1739.

3 CROSS, GUSTAV. "Another Donne Allusion." Notes and Queries
   205:532-33.
      Cites Donne's opening line of "Twicknam Gardens, "Blasted
   with sights, and surrounded with tears," as the source of
   Love in a Tub (IV.v.41): "Blasted with sighs, and almost
   drown'd in years."

4 DOBRÉE, BONAMY. "Etherege." In Restoration Comedy, 1660-1720.
   London: Oxford University Press, pp. 58-77.
      Reprint of 1924.B2.

5 VIETH, DAVID M. "Etherege's 'Man of Mode' and Rochester's
   'Artemisa to Cloe.'" Notes and Queries 203:473-74.
      Notes the parallels between the poem and the play in four
   ideas: 1) a fop is the product of art and education, 2) women
   prefer fools to wits as lovers, 3) the wit pries into secrets
   better left alone, 4) the fool who mistakes appearance for

reality is happy in the deception. These "parallel ideas may
have been formulated during casual conversation between the
two men."

<u>1959</u>

A BOOKS

1 ETHEREGE, GEORGE. <u>The Man of Mode; or, Sir Fopling Flutter</u>. In
<u>Plays of the Restoration and Eighteenth Century</u>. Edited by
Dougald Macmillan and Howard Mumford Jones. New York: Holt,
Rinehart and Winston, pp. 82-129.
Reprint of 1938.A1; see 1931.A2.

2 ETHEREGE, GEORGE. <u>The Man of Mode; or, Sir Fopling Flutter</u>. In
<u>Six Restoration Plays</u>. Edited by John Harold Wilson. River-
side Edition. Boston: Houghton-Mifflin, pp. vii-xiv, 87-167.

B SHORTER WRITINGS

1 BERKELEY, DAVID S. <u>The Précieuse, or Distressed Heroine of</u>
<u>Restoration Comedy</u>. Arts and Sciences Studies, Humanities
Series, no. 6. Oklahoma State University, Publications, 56:19.
Stillwater, Okla.: Oklahoma State University, 21 pp.
Cites Aurelia in <u>Love in a Tub</u> as one type of distressed
heroine.

2 CECIL, C. D. "Libertine and Précieux Elements in Restoration
Comedy." <u>Essays in Criticism</u> 9:239-53.
Understanding précieux elements allows us to see the male
protagonist as one who must compromise between libertinism
and self-control, between intellectual vitality and physical
restraint. Special attention to <u>The Man of Mode</u>.

3 HOLLAND, NORMAN N. <u>The First Modern Comedies: The Significance</u>
<u>of Etherege, Wycherley, and Congreve</u>. Cambridge, Mass.:
Harvard University Press, pp. 20-37, 86-95.
Makes three generalizations on language and action that
can be applied to Restoration "anti-heroic comedies": 1) love
is accompanied by hostility or reluctance, 2) abstracts and
ideals resolve into physical realities, 3) outer appearance
and inner nature are inconsistent. <u>She Wou'd if She Cou'd</u>
involves a series of contrasts; <u>The Man of Mode</u> develops two
parallel lines of intrigue. See Ph.D. Diss., 1956.B4. See also
1957.B4. Reprinted in 1967.B6.

*4 SIMON, IRENE. "Pride of Reason in the Restoration." <u>Revue des</u>
<u>Langues Vivantes</u> 25:375-96, 453-73.

1959

In Donald F. Bond, <u>The Age of Dryden</u>. Goldentree Bibliography Series. Northbrook, Ill.: AMH, p. 52, no. 5.

5 VIETH, DAVID M. "Order of Contents as Evidence of Authorship:
Rochester's <u>Poems</u> of 1680." <u>Papers of the Bibliographical
Society of America</u> 53:293-308.
Demonstrates that the two verse exchanges with Buckhurst
are by Etherege, not Rochester. See 1680.B2; see also Thorpe,
1963.A1, pp. 79-85.

1960

A BOOKS--NONE

B SHORTER WRITINGS

1 AVERY, EMMETT L., ed. <u>The London Stage, Part 2: 1700-1729</u>. 2
vols. Carbondale: Southern Illinois Univ. Press. Vol. 1:
clxxviii (intro.) + 460 (calendar) + clxxix-ccxii (index);
Vol. 2: xiv + 461-1044 (calendar) + xv-xliii (index).
"A Calendar of Plays, Entertainments and Afterpieces
Together with Casts, Box-Receipts and Contemporary Comment
Compiled from the Playbills, Newspapers, and Theatrical Diaries
of the Period." References to productions of Etherege's plays
from 1700-29. Introduction reprinted in 1968.B3.

*2 BARRON, LEON O. "The Quest for the Good Society, Friends and
Families in Restoration Comedy." Dissertation, Harvard
University.
In McNamee.

3 DAICHES, DAVID. "The Restoration." In <u>A Critical History of
English Literature</u>. 4 vols. London: Secker and Warburg;
New York: Roland Press, 3:540-42.
<u>Love in a Tub</u> is not strong in plot, but provides a "com-
petitive sophistication." <u>She Wou'd if She Cou'd</u> "establishes
a satisfactory <u>modus vivendi</u> between wit and virtue." <u>The Man
of Mode</u>, Etherege's "most brilliant comedy," adds new notes of
bargaining and wit combat, balancing desire and prudence,
surrender and freedom.

4 PORTE, MICHAEL SELDON. "The Servant in Restoration Comedy." Dissertation, Northwestern University, 204 pp.
"Examines sociological position of domestic servant in
Restoration England, compares servants in adaptations with
their prototypes, and relates these findings . . . to approxi-
mately sixty Restoration comedies. Shows that the stereotype
is an over-simplification of conditions in real life . . ."

DA, 21 (1961):3093.

5 TATUM, NANCY R. "Attitudes toward the Country in Restoration
  Comedy, 1660-1728." Dissertation, Bryn Mawr. 134 pp.
      The unchanging country patterns of life are ridiculed by
  "the town's endless pursuit of fashion and variety." DA, 21
  (1961):3452.

6 TAVE, STUART M. The Amiable Humorist: A Study in the Comic
  Theory and Criticism of the Eighteenth and Nineteenth Centuries.
  Chicago: University of Chicago Press, 304 pp.
      Sees a change from the "vituperative wit" of Etherege's
  protagonist Dorimant to Congreve's good-natured heroes.

1961

A BOOKS--NONE

B SHORTER WRITINGS

1 ENGEL, CLAIRE-ELIANE. "Bussy-Rabutin et Sir George Etherege."
  Revue des Sciences Humaines 103:417:19.
      Finds Etherege's knowledge of Histoire Amoureuse des Gaules
  (translated in IV.i of The Man of Mode as The Loves of France)
  extraordinary, and speculates that Etherege might have met
  the author, Roger de Rabutin, Comte de Bussy (1618-93), when
  Etherege was in France.

2 HOY, CYRUS. "The Effect of the Restoration on Drama." Tennessee
  Studies in Literature 6:85-91.
      Argues that "there is no room for compassion in comedies
  of manners, which may be one of the limitations of the form.
  When compassion for Society's follies and vices enters the
  satiric picture, sentiment enters with it . . ." Leads to a
  comparison of Dorimant and Bevil, Jr., in The Conscious Lovers.

3 KRUTCH, JOSEPH WOOD. Comedy and Conscience after the Restoration.
  New York: Columbia University Press, pp. 18-19, 174-76,
  passim.
      Reprint of 1924.B3, with index and updated bibliography
  by G. S. Alleman.

4 SCOUTEN, ARTHUR H., ed. The London Stage, Part 3: 1729-1747.
  2 vols. Carbondale: Southern Illinois University Press.
  Vol. 1: clxxxviii (intro.) + 596 (calendar) + clxxxix-
  ccxxiii (index); Vol. 2: xiv + 597-1315 (calendar) + xv-lii
  (index).
      See 1960.B1; introduction reprinted in 1968.B16.

1961

5 SHARMA, R. C. "Conventions of Speech in Restoration Comedy of
  Manners." Indian Journal of English Studies 2:24-38.
     Restoration comedy has dual aspects--its roots are in life
  and it is chiseled by art. Classifies types of language used
  in the plays, and concludes that the style of Restoration
  comedy fits its purpose and content.

*6 SUERBAUM, ULRICH. Die Entwicklung englischen Restaurations-
  kömodie (1660-72). Habilitations-schrift, Maschinenschrift,
  Münster.
     Noted in Germer, 1963.B2.

1962

A BOOKS

1 AIKEN, W. RALPH, JR. "Nature to Advantage Dress'd: A Study of
  Sir George Ethrege as Playwright." Dissertation, Duke
  University, 216 pp.
     Traces the development of Etherege as a playwright, taking
  up the plays chronologically. DA, 23 (1963):3349.

2 ETHEREGE, GEORGE. Możność chęciom niedostala [She Wou'd if She
  Cou'd]. In Angielska Komedia Restauracji. Introduction by
  Grzegorz Sinko. Wroclaw and Warszawa: Zaklad Narodowy.
     Introduction comments on Etherege's life and works (pp.
  xxi-xxviii) followed by text with notes. In Polish.

3 _____. The Man of Mode; or, Sir Fopling Flutter. Edited by
  Bernard F. Dukore. San Francisco: Chandler Publishing,
  xviii + 99 pp.

4 _____. The Man of Mode; or, Sir Fopling Flutter. In Plays of the
  Restoration and Eighteenth Century. Edited by Dougald
  Macmilan and Howard Mumford Jones. New York: Holt, Rinehart,
  and Winston, pp. 82-129.
     Reprint of 1938.A1; see 1931.A2; 1959.A1.

5 _____. The Man of Mode; or, Sir Fopling Flutter. In Restoration
  Plays. Revised Edition. Introduction by Edmund Gosse.
  London: Dent (Everyman's Library); New York: Dutton, pp.
  434-509.
     Reprint of 1932.A1.

B SHORTER WRITINGS

1 DOBRÉE, BONAMY. "Etherege." In Restoration Comedy, 1660-1720.
  London: Oxford University Press, pp. 58-77.

1962

Reprint of 1924.B2.

2 DRYDEN, JOHN. "Preface of the Translator to 'A Parallel betwixt Painting and Poetry': De Arte Graphica by C. A. Du Fresnoy." In Of Dramatic Poesy and other Critical Essays. 2 vols. Edited by George Watson. London: Dent (Everyman's Library), 2:198.

In a note, Watson suggests the poet referred to is Etherege. See 1695.B1.

3 GIBB, CARSON. "Figurative Structure in Restoration Comedy." Dissertation, University of Pennsylvania, 342 pp.

Treats all of Etherege's plays, as well as selected comedies by Dryden and Wycherley. Finds a figurative structure resulting from the juxtaposition of apparently unrelated actions. These various actions can be reduced to two motives: "love of pleasure and love of power." DA, 23 (1962):4683-84.

4 KNIGHT, G. WILSON. The Golden Labyrinth: A Study of British Drama. London: Phoenix House, pp. 131-35.

Sees in Dorimant's cynicism "a certain unease and even guilt . . . . Our pleasure derives from a complicated poetic recognition" of this duality.

5 NORRELL, LEMUEL N. "The Cuckold in Restoration Comedy." Dissertation, Florida State University, 163 pp.

Observes that the cuckold is "the scapegoat of Restoration comedy." DA, 23 (1963):3889.

6 PETERSON, WILLIAM M. and MORTON, RICHARD. "Mirrors on the Restoration Stage." Notes and Queries, 207:10-13, 63-67.

Two-part article classifying the various uses of mirrors on the stage from 1660-1700. Sir Fopling, they note, observes himself, thus reinforcing vanity and conceit. These scenes illustrate the narcissistic tendencies of such characters.

7 STONE, GEORGE WINCHESTER, JR., ed. The London Stage, Part 4: 1747-1776. 3 vols. Carbondale: Southern Illinois University Press. Vol. 1: ccxii (intro.) + 492 (calendar) + ccxiii-cclxxviii (index); Vol. 2: xvi + 493-1266 (calendar) + xvii-lxvi (index); Vol. 3: xvi + 1267-1994 (calendar) + xvii-lxv (index).

See 1960.B1; introduction reprinted in 1968.B17.

8 VERNON, PAUL F. "Marriage of Convenience and the Moral Code of Restoration Comedy." Essays in Criticism 12:370-87.

Argues that Restoration comedy has a wholly consistent moral standpoint and that modern critics, such as Wain (1956.

1963

B8, 1957.B7), Knights (1937.B1), and Leech (1951.B4), have been misled by their failure to take into account the marriage of convenience in the period. Cites The Man of Mode as the finest comic handling of libertinism that, in the end, gives way to the power of love.

1963

A BOOKS

1 ETHEREGE, GEORGE. The Poems. Edited by James Thorpe. Princeton: Princeton University Press, 149 pp.
    The standard edition of the poetry of Etherege. Included are 31 poems by Etherege, three answers to verse epistles by Dryden and Buckhurst, and six poems of doubtful authorship. Extensive notes and full bibliographical apparatus.

B SHORTER WRITINGS

1 ANON. "The Poetic Romp." TLS, 18 October, p. 826.
    Review of Thorpe's edition of Etherege's poetry (1963.A1). "Etherege's value as a writer still rests mainly on his command of style."

2 GERMER, ERICH. "Sentimentale Züge in den Lustspielgesalten Ethereges, Wycherleys, Congreves, Vanbrughs, und Farquhars." Inaugural Dissertation, Münster, 165 pp.
    Takes up each play separately, noting the occurrence and handling of sentimentalism in the five playwrights. In the plays of Etherege (pp. 35-49), Germer finds most sentimentalism expressed in the "love and honor" plot of Love in a Tub.

3 LORD, GEORGE de FOREST, ed. Poems on Affairs of State: Augustan Satirical Verse, 1660-1714. Vol. 1: 1660-1678. New Haven: Yale University Press.
    Includes a number of poems that mention Etherege. With detailed commentary. See 1680.B2; 1682.B1; 1697.B1; 1705.B1.

4 QUAINTANCE, RICHARD E. "French Sources of the Restoration 'Imperfect Enjoyment' Poem." Philological Quarterly 42:190-99.
    Provides the French source, Charles Beys (1610-59), "La Iovissance Imparfaite," from which Etherege adapted his poem "The Imperfect Enjoyment." Notes where Etherege follows his source closely and where he alters it, going away from it at the end of his poem to bring out a paradox.

5 SIMON, IRENE. "Restoration Comedy and the Critics." Revue des Langues Vivantes 29:397-430.

1964

After a general review of the criticism of Restoration comedy, ending with specific attention to Underwood (1957.A1) and Holland (1959.B3), Simon then provides her own reading of The Man of Mode, using Holland as a springboard. She argues that Dorimant is not a reformed rake but is checked in his career and beaten at his own game. Etherege, thus, exposes the aggressive libertine creed.

*6 SINGH, SARUP. The Theory of the Drama in the Restoration Period. Calcutta: Orient Longmans.
    Cited in several reviews as dramatic theory evolved through dedications, prefaces, prologues, and epilogues. See Barnard, 1975.B1; is this a revision of 1953.B2?

7 TIEDJE, EGON. "Die Tradition Ben Jonsons in der Restaurations komödie." Dissertation, Hamburg. (published in the series "Britannica et Americana," Band 11. Hamburg: Cram, deGruyter.)
    Cites influences of Jonson in the characters, forms, and techniques of Restoration comedy, including all of Etherege's plays.

8 WALL, DONALD CLARK. "The Restoration Rake in Life and Comedy." Dissertation, Florida State University, 232 pp.
    Comparing history and drama, Wall determines that most comedies (of the 16 examined, including all those by Etherege) "are not realistic." He does find Etherege's first two plays faithfully presenting life, whereas The Man of Mode is "atypical." DA, 25 (1964):458.

1964

A BOOKS

1 ETHEREGE, GEORGE. The Man of Mode; or, Sir Fopling Flutter. In Plays of the Restoration and Eighteenth Century. Edited by Dougald Macmillan and Howard Mumford Jones. New York: Holt, Rinehart, and Winston, pp. 82-129.
    Reprint of 1938.A1; see 1931.A2; 1959.A1; 1967.A4.

2 MEINDL, VINCENZ. Sir George Etheredge, Sein Leben, Seine Zeit und Seine Dramen. (Wiener Beiträge zur englischen Philologie, 14.) Wien und Leipzig: Bramüller; New York: Johnson Reprints, 278 pp.
    Reprint of 1901.A1.

1964

B SHORTER WRITINGS

*1 GILDE, JOSEPH M. "Rakes and Fools; a Study of the Development of
     the Libertine-Satiric Tradition in Restoration Comedy, 1660-
     1676." Dissertation, University of Chicago.
        In McNamee.

2 HAYMAN, JOHN GRIFFITHS. "Raillery during the Restoration Period
     and Early Eighteenth Century." Dissertation, Northwestern
     University, 209 pp.
        Studies "prevalence of both affable and satiric raillery,"
     the use of raillery in satire, and the change of concept in
     the use of raillery from Dryden to Swift. DA, 25 (1965):
     4146-47.

3 HOY, CYRUS. "The Pleasures and the Perils of Deception." In
     The Hyacinth Room: An Investigation into the Nature of
     Comedy, Tragedy, and Tragicomedy. London: Chatto and Windus,
     pp. 119-85.
        Deals with characters facing the problem of changed circum-
     stances. Examples from several Restoration comedies, includ-
     ing The Man of Mode.

4 HYMAS, SCOTT SIMPSON. "The Satiric Attitude: Rejection in the
     Comedies of Wycherley and Etherege." Dissertation, Western
     Reserve University, 408 pp.
        "The plays of Etherege and Wycherley are more expressive
     of the rejection of the satiric attitude than the acceptance
     of the comic." Deals with all of Etherege's plays. DA, 25
     (1965):6594.

5 KNIGHTS, L. C. "Restoration Comedy: The Reality and the Myth."
     In Explorations: Essays in Criticism Mainly on the Literature
     of the Seventeenth Century. Harmondsworth, Middlesex: Penguin,
     pp. 139-57.
        Reprint of essay, 1937.B1; reprint of collection, 1946.B2.

*6 LOVE, HAROLD H. R. "Satire in the Drama of the Restoration."
     Dissertation, University of Cambridge.
        In McNamee. Jordan (1972.B9) notes the extended investi-
     gation of carnival elements in Restoration drama. Love also
     deals with "plot motifs rather than character types . . .
     The comic release seems to be primarily from Puritan/political
     pressures rather than neo-classic social restraints."

7 McDONALD, CHARLES O. "Restoration Comedy as Drama of Satire: An
     Investigation into Seventeenth-Century Aesthetics." Studies
     in Philology 61:522-44.

In Restoration comedy, there are no heroes and heroines, just protagonists and antagonists. Thus, because the plays avoid these preconceptions, they are the "most complexly and consciously moral comedies." Extended discussion of <u>The Man of Mode</u> brings out some subtle features of the play, particularly the satire.

8 WILCOX, JOHN. "Etherege." In <u>The Relation of Molière to Restoration Comedy</u>. New York: Benjamin Blom, pp. 70-81. Reprint of 1938.B2.

9 WILKINSON, D. R. M. <u>The Comedy of Habit: An Essay on the Use of Courtesy Literature in a Study of Restoration Comedy</u>. Leidse Germanistische en Anglistiche Reeks van de Rijksuniversiteit te Leiden, 4. Leiden: Universitaire Pers, xii + 188 pp., passim.

Uses Francis Osborne's <u>Advice to a Son</u> (1656-58) and other contemporary courtesy literature to comment on the characterization of the gallant. Finds that wit "is the product of habit rather than an expression of creative art . . ."

<u>1965</u>

A BOOKS--NONE

B SHORTER WRITINGS

1 HARRIS, BERNARD. "The Dialectic of those Frantic Times." In <u>Restoration Theatre</u>. Edited by John Russell Brown and Bernard Harris. Stratford-upon-Avon Studies, no. 6. London: Edward Arnold; New York: St. Martin's Press, pp. 10-40, see especially pp. 28-32.

Claims that Etherege and Congreve are "the true prose stylists of the comedy of manners." Harris focuses on <u>The Man of Mode</u>, showing how in references to fruit and vegetables, Etherege's "similitudes from natural life offer a relationship to the human, not a distinction or even a parallel."

*2 JORDAN, R. J. "The Libertine Gentleman in Restoration Comedy." Dissertation, Univ. of London.
      In McNamee.

*3 POTTER, L. D. "The Fop and Related Figures in Drama from Jonson to Cibber." Dissertation, Cambridge.
      In McNamee.

4 PINTO, VIVIAN de SOLA. <u>The Restoration Court Poets</u>. British Writers and their Work, no. 186. London: British Council,

1965

pp. 33-39.
Discusses Etherege's poetry. When Etherege is at his best,
Pinto admires his craftsmanship and his ability to speak in
other voices than that of a court gallant. The "light verse"
contains "gaiety, insouciance, and [an] attractive mixture of
innocence and sophistication."

5 POWELL, JOCELYN. "George Ethrege and the Form of a Comedy." In
Restoration Theatre. Stratford-upon-Avon Studies, no. 6.
Edited by John Russell Brown and Bernard Harris. London:
Edward Arnold; New York: St. Martin's Press, pp. 43-69.
Argues that Etherege builds "his dramatic interest on the
tensions of conversation rather than suspense of plot." Thus,
"form has become a means of expressing experience, rather than
idea," and ultimately "the comedy of judgment gives way to the
comedy of experience." Detailed comments on all the plays.
Reprinted in 1966.B14; 1973.A2.

6 SHARMA, RAM CHANDRA. Themes and Conventions in the Comedy of
Manners. London: Asia Publishing House, 354 pp.
Characters are classified into three patterns: 1) Gay
and Wild, 2) Fops and Fools, 3) Grotesques. Examines the
Restoration conventions in language and action, followed by
the changes in "breaking the pattern" of these conventions.
Earlier article (1961.B5) revised into the chapter on language.

7 The Spectator. 5 vols. Edited with an introduction and notes by
Donald F. Bond. Oxford: Clarendon Press.
Annotated edition of Spectator pages. For 1711.B1, see
1:185-91; for 1711.B3, see 1:215-20; for 1711.B4, see 1:278-80;
for 1711.B5, see 1:322-25.

8 TAYLOR, CHARLENE MAE. "Aspects of Social Criticism in Restoration Comedy." Dissertation, University of Illinois. 263 pp.
Considers "the satiric use of the figure of the social
climber from 1660-1708." Etherege included in the second
chapter, where social climbers are shamed into proper behavior.
DA, 26 (1966):7301-2.

9 VAN LENNEP, WILLIAM, ed. The London Stage, Part I: 1660-1700.
Critical introduction by Emmett L. Avery and Arthur H. Scouten.
Carbondale: Southern Illinois University Press, clxxvi
(intro.) + 532 (calendar) + clxxvii-ccxcii (index). See
1960.B1; 1968.B2. Revision in progress by Scouten, R. D.
Hume, and Judith Milhous.

10 WILSON, JOHN HAROLD. A Preface to Restoration Drama. Boston:
Houghton-Mifflin, pp. 169-77, passim.

1966

Classifies types of drama in the period; The Man of Mode
considered "comedy of wit." Divides characters by their
language: "Etherege maintains his characters as much by their
quality of speech as by their substance. His true wits talk
in sharp, precise, often balanced or periodic, sentences,
wasting no words and rarely using the commonplace, interjec-
tions of ordinary speech . . ." Reprinted in 1968.B18.

1966

A BOOKS

1 ETHEREGE, GEORGE. The Man of Mode; or, Sir Fopling Flutter.
      Edited by W. B. Carnochan. Regents Restoration Drama Series.
   Lincoln: University of Nebraska Press, xxi + 158 pp.
         Introduction treats the uncertain ending in the light of
   Dorimant's character; he is rewarded, but he has suffered
   embarrassment. The play achieves a precarious balance "between the order of comedy and the disorder of things as they
   are."

2 ETHEREGE, GEORGE. The Man of Mode; or, Sir Fopling Flutter.   In
   Restoration Plays. Introduction by Brice Harris. New York:
   Random House/Modern Library, pp. vii-xviii, 155-243.
         Reprint of 1953.A2.

B SHORTER WRITINGS

1 AUFFRET, J. M. "The Man of Mode and The Plain Dealer: Common
      Origins and Parallels." Etudes Anglaises 19:209-22.
         Conjectures about the real life prototypes in both plays,
   the common connection being Moll Kirke (the Loveit episode in
   The Man of Mode and the Olivia portion of The Plain Dealer)
   and her relationship with John Sheffield, Earl of Mulgrave.

2 BATESON, F. W. "L. C. Knights and Restoration Comedy." In
      Restoration Drama: Modern Essays in Criticism. Edited by
   John Loftis. New York: Oxford University Press, pp. 22-31.
         Reprint of 1957.B2.

3 BOYETTE, P. E. "The Songs of Etherege." Studies in English
      Literature 6:409-19.
         Traces the use of the songs in the plays, finding them
   germane to the structure of the whole. The songs, moreover,
   contribute to the characterization, reveal an emotional
   attitude, help distinguish a theme, or satirize a traditional
   ideology, motif, or character.

1966

4 BRETT-SMITH, H. F. B. "Introduction to The Dramatic Works of Sir
   George Etherege." In Restoration Drama: Modern Essays in
   Criticism. Edited by John Loftis. New York: Oxford Univer-
   sity Press, pp. 44-56.
       Reprint of pp. lxix-lxxxiii in 1927.A1.

5 CECIL, C. D. "Delicate and Indelicate Puns in Restoration
   Comedy." Modern Language Review 61:572-78.
       Restoration comedy if full of puns without its audience
   thinking the worse of it, but Dennis and Addison lead the
   early eighteenth-century polemics against this rhetorical
   figure. Cecil notes that in literature and in life, playwrights enjoyed puns. Cites Etherege's letter (1928.A1, p.
   189), where he regrets his inability to find a good quibble
   for his London friends.

6 _____. "'Une Espèce D'Eloquence Abrégée': The Idealized Speech
   of Restoration Comedy." Etudes Anglaises 19:15-25.
       Focuses on refined speech: "Certain attitudes need care-
   ful shading." The wits avoid jargon, and their figurative
   usages are "economical, precise, and unusual all at once."
   Fashionable language, thus, creates idealized speech manners.

7 _____. "Raillery in Restoration Comedy." Huntington Library
   Quarterly 29:147-59.
       Raillery tests the honesty of characters, as in Harriet's
   early challenges to Dorimant, or in Medley's ironic remarks
   to Dorimant on the campaign against Loveit. Understanding
   this verbal decorum, the audience can distinguish the honnête
   railleur from the fool.

8 CUNNINGHAM, JOHN E. Restoration Drama. Literature in Perspective
   Series. London: Evans Bros., pp. 40-58.
       A brief biography followed by a discussion of each play.
   Love in a Tub is too fragmented with its "two" plots; She Wou'd
   if She Cou'd is poorly constructed, though local color and
   dialogue provide some interest. The Man of Mode, however, is
   Etherege's triumph, and Dorimant leaves us with a slightly sad
   remembrance of his ruthlessness and his honesty.

9 ELWIN, MALCOM. "Etherege." In The Playgoer's Handbook to Restoration Drama. Port Washington, N. Y.: Kennikat Press, pp.
   60-68.
       Reprint of 1928.B2.

10 EMERY, JOHN P. "Restoration Dualism of the Court Writers."
   Revue des Langues Vivantes, 32:238-65.
       Shows how plays support what is known about the real lives

82

of several courtiers, including Etherege. Defining dualism
as public virtue and private vice, Emery finds both in
Etherege's life and plays, especially Love in a Tub and The
Man of Mode.

11 KNIGHTS, L. C. "Restoration Comedy: The Reality and the Myth."
In Restoration Drama: Modern Essays in Criticism. Edited by
John Loftis. New York: Oxford University Press, pp. 3-31.
Reprint of 1937.B1.

12 LEGOUIS, P., et al. "Les Voies de la Critique Récente: Comment
elle étudie la comédie de la Restauration." Etudes Anglaises
19:412-23.
A review of recent (since 1945) criticism on Restoration
comedy, stressing originality of Holland (1959.B3), Fujimura
(1952.B1), and Underwood (1957.A1).

13 LOFTIS, JOHN, ed. Restoration Drama: Modern Essays in Criticism.
New York: Oxford University Press, xi + 371 pp.
Brief introduction to essays in the collection, including
1966.B2, B4, B11, B16, B22.

14 MINER, EARL R., ed. Restoration Dramatists: A Collection of
Critical Essays. Twentieth-Century Views. Englewood Cliffs,
N. J.: Prentice-Hall, ix + 179 pp.
Introduces essays, citing "common elements and resem-
blances," and notes "fruitful approaches." See 1966.B17, B23.

15 MOHANTY, HARENDRA PRASAD. "Restoration Comedy: A Revaluation."
Literary Criterion (Mysore, India), 7:21-27.
Compares Restoration comedy with a Donne sermon, with
Shakespeare, and with Ben Jonson. Finds nothing intellectual
and only the crudest verbal wit.

16 MONTGOMERY, GUY. "The Challenge of Restoration Comedy." In
Restoration Drama: Modern Essays in Criticism. Edited by
John Loftis. New York: Oxford University Press, pp. 32-43.
Reprint of 1929.B3.

17 POWELL, JOCELYN. "George Etherege and the Form of a Comedy."
In Restoration Dramatists: A Collection of Critical Essays.
Edited by Earl R. Miner. Twentieth-Century Views. Englewood
Cliffs, N. J.: Prentice-Hall, pp. 65-85.
Reprint of 1965.B5.

18 RIDDELL, JAMES ALLEN. "The Evolution of the Humours Character in
Seventeenth-Century English Comedy." Dissertation, University
of Southern California, 256 pp.

1966

Traces humours characters from Jonson to Farquhar, and
finds a widely differing attitude of the major playwrights.
"Etherege, for instance, seemed to care very little about them
[humours characters]." DA, 27 (1966):1037A-38A.

19 SCOUTEN, A. H. "Notes Toward a History of Restoration Comedy."
Philological Quarterly 45:62-70.
Argues for two distinct periods of manners comedy: 1)
1668-76 and 2) 1691-1707. Etherege and Wycherley differ
markedly from Congreve, Vanbrugh, Farquhar, and Southerne:
the earlier plays concentrate on pre-marriage, the latter ones
generally deal with post-marriage. Scouten also notes the
kinds of plays popular before comedy of manners: musical
drama, topical political satire, romance intrigue, and heroic
drama.

20 SPENCE, JOSEPH. Observations, Anecdotes and Characters of Books
and Men. 2 vols. Edited by James M. Osborn. Oxford:
Clarendon Press, 2:638 (An Appendix to entry no. 678).
Discusses the various identifications of real life persons
thought to be the models for characters in The Man of Mode.

21 TRAUGOTT, JOHN. "The Rake's Progress from Court to Comedy: A
Study in Comic Form." Studies in English Literature 6:381-
407.
Because Restoration comedy grows out of heroic drama, the
rake-hero redefines love and honor, naturally and cynically.
The questioning of reality forces the libertine to sort out
social values. Traces the rake-hero through Etherege's
comedies.

22 UNDERWOOD, DALE. "The Comic Values--The Man of Mode." From
Etherege and Seventeenth-Century Comedy of Manners. In Res-
toration Drama: Modern Essays in Criticism. Edited by John
Loftis. New York: Oxford University Press, pp. 57-81.
Reprint of Chapter 5 in 1957.A1.

23 _____. "The Comic Language." From Etherege and Seventeenth-
Century Comedy of Manners. In Restoration Dramatists: A
Collection of Critical Essays. Twentieth-Century Views.
Edited by Earl R. Miner. Englewood Cliffs, N. J.: Prentice-
Hall, pp. 87-103.
Reprint of Chapter 6 in 1957.A1.

1967

A BOOKS

1 ETHEREGE, GEORGE. The Man of Mode; or, Sir Fopling Flutter.
Selected scenes in L'Humour en Angleterre, Anthologie du Moyen
Age au Debut de l'Ere Classique. Introduced and Translated
by A. Maurocordato. Paris: Collection Bilenque Aubier, pp.
352-63, 418-23.
The Man of Mode, II.ii; I.i.

*2 _____. The Man of Mode; or, Sir Fopling Flutter. In Plays,
Classical and Contemporary. Edited by Richard Wald Lid and
Daniel Bernd. Philadelphia: Lippincott, 623 pp.

B SHORTER WRITINGS

1 BIRDSALL, VIRGINIA OGDEN. "The English Comic Spirit on the Res-
toration Stage." Dissertation, Brown University, 328 pp.
Sees heros and heroines of Etherege, Wycherley, and
Congreve "as genuinely comic and wholly English figures."
Etherege's comic vision is perhaps the purest. DA, 28 (1968):
3137A. See book, 1970.B2.

2 BRACHER, FREDERICK. "The Letterbooks of Sir George Etherege."
Harvard Library Bulletin 15:238-45.
Shows how the Harvard letters (fMS Thr. 11 and fMS Thr.
11.1) differ from the letterbook in the BM (Add. Mss. 11513)
kept by Etherege's unscrupulous secretary, Hugo Hughes, at
Ratisbon. The Harvard letters are Sir George's own copies
carried with him to Paris after the Revolution of 1689.

3 _____. "Sir George Etherege and his Secretary." Harvard Library
Bulletin 15:331-44.
Demonstrates that Etherege's secretary in Ratisbon, Hugo
Hughes, was in league with the Dutch resident there. Hughes
was, consequently, giving Stuart secrets away to the cause of
William of Orange, for which he expected to be rewarded with
the post of resident upon Etherege's departure. Ironically,
William Harbord, Hughes's patron, was inadvertently the cause
of the cashiering of Hughes in 1693.

4 BROICH, ULRICH. "Libertin und Heroischer Held: Das Drama der
Englischen Restaurationzeit und Seine Leitbilder." Anglia
85:34-57.
Posits that the heroic and comic heroes have the same
roots. And these heroic and comic characteristics extend to
the themes and structures of the plays. Wit in comedy is

1967

    equated to honor in tragedy. <u>Love in a Tub</u> is a primary
    example.

5 DOBRÉE, BONAMY. "His Excellency Sir George Etherege." In <u>Essays</u>
   <u>in Biography, 1680-1726</u>. London: Oxford University Press,
   pp. 1-56.
      Reprint of 1925.B1.

6 HOLLAND, NORMAN N. <u>The First Modern Comedies: The Significance</u>
   <u>of Etherege, Wycherley, and Congreve</u>. Bloomington, Ind.:
   Indiana University Press, pp. 20-37, 86-95.
      Reprint of 1959.B3.

7 LOTT, JAMES DAVID. "Restoration Comedy: The Critical View,
   1913-1965." Dissertation, University of Wisconsin. 446 pp.
      Takes up various critical responses to Restoration comedy
   beginning with Palmer (1913.B3). Includes relevant criticism
   on Etherege. <u>DA</u>, 28 (1968):2688A.

8 SHERBURN, GEORGE, and BOND, DONALD F. "Restoration and Eighteenth
   Century." In <u>A Literary History of England</u>. New York:
   Appleton-Century-Crofts, pp. 763-66.
      Reprint of 1948.B2 with bibliography updated by Bond.

9 WILSON, JOHN HAROLD. <u>The Court Wits of the Restoration</u>. New
   York Octagon Press, 264 pp., passim.
      Reprint of 1948.B4.

<u>1968</u>

A BOOKS

*1 ETHEREGE, GEORGE. <u>The Man of Mode; or, Sir Fopling Flutter</u>. In
   <u>Restoration Drama</u>. Edited by Eugene Waith. New York: Bantam
   Books.

2 _____. <u>The Man of Mode; or, Sir Fopling Flutter</u>. In <u>Three Res-</u>
   <u>toration Comedies</u>. Edited by Gāmini Salgādo. Harmondsworth,
   Middlesex: Penguin, pp. 28-33, 43-146.

3 YOUNG, PETER BAXTER. "The Plays of Sir George Etherege: A
   Production-Oriented Approach." Dissertation, Stanford University, 205 pp.
      Suggests ways in which directors can understand and pro-
   duce Etherege's plays on stage. One chapter alloted to each
   of the plays. <u>DA</u>, 29 (1969):2388A.

B SHORTER WRITINGS

1 AUFFRET, J. "Etherege à la école de Molière." In <u>Dramaturgie
   et Société: Rapports entre l'oeuvre théâtrale, son inter-
   pretation et son public aux 16e et 17e siècles</u>. Edited by
   Jean Jaquot, Elie Konigson, and Marcel Oddon. 2 vols. Paris:
   Editions du Centre National de la Recherche Scientifique, 1:
   395-407.
       Believes that as many as five of Molière's plays may have
   influenced Etherege. In <u>The Man of Mode</u>, Etherege retained
   Molière's stylization but was pushed to greater verisimilitude.

2 AVERY, EMMETT L. and SCOUTEN, ARTHUR H. <u>The London Stage, 1660-
   1700: A Critical Introduction</u>. Carbondale: Southern
   Illinois University Press, clxxvii pp.
       Reprint of critical introduction from 1965.B8.

3 AVERY, EMMETT L. <u>The London Stage, 1700-1729: A Critical
   Introduction</u>. Carbondale: Southern Illinois University Press,
   cxcii pp.
       Reprint of critical introduction from 1960.B1.

4 CONAGHAN, JOHN. "A Prompt Copy of Etherege's <u>Man of Mode</u>."
   <u>Library Review</u> 21:387-88.
       Discovery of a marked, prompt copy of the first quarto
   in the National Library of Scotland. The cast, led by Clark
   and Goodman, may have acted <u>The Man of Mode</u> in Edinburgh in
   1679 after leaving London.

5 COX, R. S., Jr. "Richard Flecknoe and <u>The Man of Mode</u>." <u>Modern
   Language Quarterly</u> 29:183-89.
       Shows that <u>A Treatise on the Sport of Wit</u> (1675) by
   Richard Flecknoe is probably the work commented on by Medley
   as <u>The Diversions of Bruxells</u> in <u>The Man of Mode</u>, II.i. Later
   in the play, Dorimant as Courtage acts the sort of person
   described in the <u>Treatise</u>.

6 FUJIMURA, THOMAS H. <u>The Restoration Comedy of Wit</u>. New York:
   Barnes and Noble, 232 pp., passim.
       Reprint of 1952.B1.

7 HAYMAN, JOHN. "Raillery in Restoration Satire." <u>Huntington
   Library Quarterly</u> 31:107-22.
       Uses observations on satire by Dryden to point out the
   social practice of raillery: 1) manner, 2) technique, 3)
   target, 4) end or intention. Although the remarks on Etherege
   are restricted to <u>The Man of Mode</u>, the topic does have implications for <u>She Wou'd if She Cou'd</u> and <u>Love in a Tub</u>. See

1968

Cecil's approach to the same topic, 1966.B7.

8 HOGAN, CHARLES BEECHER, ed. The London Stage, Part 5: 1776–1800.
   3 vols. Carbondale: Southern Illinois University Press.
   Vol. 1: ccxviii (intro.) + 632 (calendar) + ccxix–cclxxxii
   (index); Vol. 2: xvi + 633–1472 (calendar) + xvii–cxviii
   (index); Vol. 3: xvi + 1473–2298 (calendar) + xvii–cxvii
   (index).
      See 1960.B1.

9 _____. The London Stage, 1776–1800: A Critical Introduction.
   Carbondale: Southern Illinois University Press, ccxxiv pp.
   Reprint of critical introduction from 1968.B8.

*10 KILEY, FREDERICK. "Sir George Etherege and the Restoration 'Code
   Hero.'" East-West Review 3 (Winter 1967–68):242–72.

*11 KISHI, TETSUO. "Joji Esardju no Tojo" [The First Play of George
   Etherege]. Studies in English Literature (Tokyo) 45:11–23.
      In Japanese. Listed MHRA Annual Bibliography. Translated
   in 1972.B10.

12 LEGOUIS, P. Andrew Marvell: Poet, Puritan, Patriot. 2d Edition.
   Oxford: Clarendon Press, pp. 203–4.
      Gives the details surrounding the publication of Mr.
   Smirke; or the Divine in Mode (1676.B2), which uses a character
   from Etherege's The Man of Mode to parody arguments then current.

13 LOVE, HAROLD. "The Satirised Characters in Poeta De Tristibus."
   Philological Quarterly 47:547–62.
      Identifies Etherege, plus other dramatists, satirized by
   an anonymous author in the Hudibrastic verse of Poeta de
   Tristibus, which is reprinted by ARS (1971.B4) with an introduction by Love.

14 NETTLETON, GEORGE H. English Drama of the Restoration and
   Eighteenth Century (1642–1780). New York: Macmillan, pp.
   73–77.
      Reprint of 1914.B1.

15 PEPYS, SAMUEL. The Diary. 11 vols. (when completed). Edited by
   Robert Latham and William Matthews. London: G. Bell;
   Berkeley: University of California Press, 1968–.
      Nine volumes of this standard edition are now out. For
   Pepys's remarks on Etherege, see 6:4; 7:347; 9:53–54; 178, 435.

1969

16 SCOUTEN, ARTHUR H. The London Stage, 1729-1747: A Critical
   Introduction. Carbondale: Southern Illinois University
   Press, cci pp.
        Reprint of critical introduction from 1961.B4.

17 STONE, GEORGE WINCHESTER, JR. The London Stage, 1747-1776: A
   Critical Introduction. Carbondale: Southern Illinois
   University Press, ccxv pp.
        Reprint of critical introduction from 1962.B7.

18 WILSON, JOHN HAROLD. A Preface to Restoration Drama. Cambridge,
   Mass.: Harvard University Press.
        Reprint of 1965.B10.

1969

A BOOKS

 1 ETHEREGE, GEORGE. The Man of Mode; or, Sir Fopling Flutter. In
   British Dramatists from Dryden to Sheridan. Edited by George
   H. Nettleton and Arthur E. Case. Revised by George W. Stone,
   Jr. Boston: Houghton-Mifflin, pp. 153-95.
        Reprint of 1939.A1, with notes and bibliography revised by
   Stone.

 2 UNDERWOOD, DALE. Etherege and Seventeenth-Century Comedy of
   Manners. [Hamden, Conn.]: Archon Books, ix + 165 pp.
        Reprint of 1957.A1.

B SHORTER WRITINGS

 1 BRACHER, FREDERICK. "Etherege as Diplomat." Harvard Library
   Bulletin 17:45-60.
        The same qualities that made Etherege a successful play-
   wright also made him a good diplomat: "a shrewd eye for
   pretense and hypocrisy, a level-headed estimate of men, a
   realistic view of human fallibility, and an easy way with
   people."

 2 DAVIES, PAUL C. "The State of Nature and the State of War: A
   Reconsideration of The Man of Mode." University of Toronto
   Quarterly 39:53-62.
        Focuses on Dorimant and Harriet as the high points of
   awareness in the play. Rejects arguments of Underwood (1957.
   A1), Holland (1959.B3), and Fujimura (1952.B1); the latter
   two feel that Dorimant will be redeemed by a good woman.
   Seeing her thus would only lead to a sentimental ending.
   Although Harriet has humbled Dorimant at the end of the play,

1969

they are <u>not</u> married. Thus the play is "uncompromisingly
tough and realistic."

3 DOWNES, JOHN. <u>Roscius Anglicanus, or an Historical Review of the
Stage . . . from 1660-1706</u>. Edited with introduction by John
Loftis. Augustan Reprint Society, no. 134. Los Angeles: W.
A. Clark Library, xiv + 76.
Reprint of 1708.B1.

4 HAYMAN, JOHN G. "Dorimant and the Comedy of a Man of Mode."
<u>Modern Language Quarterly</u> 30:183-97.
Believes that Dorimant is caught between social require-
ments and impulses of his nature, thus his final position in
the play is ambivalent. Praises Etherege for showing the
complex (and comic) relationship "between man's impulses and
emotions and their expression in an elaborate society."

5 KOONCE, HOWARD LEE. "Comic Values and Comic Form: The Restora-
tion Comedy of Manners in its Tradition." Dissertation,
University of Pennsylvania. 188 pp.
Traces Restoration comic tradition to Roman comedy. Deals
with stock plots, stock characters, wit, and foppery in <u>The
Man of Mode</u>. <u>DAI</u>, 30 (1969):4990A.

6 KRAUSE, DAVID. "The Defaced Angel: A Concept of Satanic Grace
in Etherege's <u>The Man of Mode</u>." <u>Drama Survey</u> 7:87-103.
Explores the attitude of comic disobedience as an act of
rebellious liberation underlying the relationship of Harriet
and Dorimant. Working from the metaphors of hell/heaven,
devil/angel, Krause explains the comic paradoxes in the
mimetic process of the theatre, where imagination triumphs
over reality.

7 KRUTCH, JOSEPH WOOD. <u>Comedy and Conscience after the Restoration</u>.
New York: Columbia University Press, pp. 18-19, 174-76, passim.
Reprint of 1924.B3, with bibliographical additions and
index prepared for the 1949 reprinting (see 1949.B1).

8 LOCKWOOD, THOMAS. "The Augustan Author-Audience Relationship:
Satiric versus Comic Forms." <u>English Literary History</u> 36:648-
58.
Deals with the problems of how an audience determines their
relation to the characters in a poem or drama (i.e., scorn or
admiration). Comedy corrects by gentle humor; satire by
sabotage through irony and parody. Medley and Dorimant, for
example, pretend to accept Sir Fopling only to trap and ridicule him. Comedy integrates society, whereas satire sets

people apart.

9 RUBIN, BARBARA L. "The Dream of Self-Fulfillment in Restoration
   Comedy: A Study in Two Parts: The Heroic Pattern in Aristo-
   phanic and Roman Comedy, and its Design and Decadence in
   English Comedy from 1660 to 1700." Dissertation, University
   of Rochester, 326 pp.
      Sees the early Restoration comedies (including those of
   Etherege) as fitting the high mimetic mode. DAI, 30 (1970):
   5419A-20A.

10 SUTHERLAND, JAMES. English Literature of the Late Seventeenth
   Century. Oxford History of English Literature. Oxford:
   Clarendon Press, pp. 105-11, 232-33.
      Praises "the unforced ease and natural rhythm" of Ether-
   ege's dialogue. Believes that Sir Fopling keeps The Man of
   Mode from becoming "a dark comedy." Etherege's letters "are
   among the most delightful of the whole period."

1970

A BOOKS

*1 ETHEREGE, GEORGE. The Man of Mode; or, Sir Fopling Flutter. In
    Classic through Modern Drama. Edited by Otto Reinert. Boston:
    Little, Brown.

*2 _____. She Wou'd if She Cou'd. In Restoration Plays. Edited by
    D. Davidson. London: Oxford University Press, 399 pp.

B SHORTER WRITINGS

1 BERMAN, RONALD. "The Comic Passions of The Man of Mode."
   Studies in English Literature 10:459-68.
      Gives the contexts of the many Waller poems quoted by
   Dorimant and shows how these lyrics of Waller underscore the
   action in The Man of Mode. At the end of the play, however,
   Waller's heroic ideals no longer apply. Dorimant and Harriet
   must find new, not conventional, ways to express their love.

2 BIRDSALL, VIRGINIA OGDEN. Wild Civility: The English Comic
   Spirit on the Restoration Stage. Bloomington, Ind.: Indiana
   University Press, pp. 40-104.
      Applies the principles of Johan Huezinga's Homo Ludens
   (i.e., "play" is a significant function of life) to Restoration comedy. Explores words, imagery, and action in each
   individual drama: Love in a Tub (pp. 40-57), She Wou'd if She
   Cou'd (pp. 57-76), and The Man of Mode (pp. 77-104). See Ph.D.

1970

Dissertation, 1967.B1.

3 BODE, ROBERT F. "A Study of the Development of the Theme of Love and Duty in English Comedy from Charles I to George I." Dissertation, University of South Carolina, 149 pp.
Traces the change of the Love/Honor theme into the Love/Duty theme in selected comedies, including those of Etherege. DAI, 31 (1971):5351A.

4 CARROLL, JOHN ELLISON. "Masking and Disguise in the Plays of Etherege, Wycherley, and Congreve." Dissertation, University of New Mexico, 261 pp.
While the mask provides spectacle, it also dramatizes other functions—"structural, thematic, symbolic, and satiric." Masking brings out structure and theme in Love in a Tub; spectacle in She Wou'd if She Cou'd; and symbol and satire in The Man of Mode. DAI, 31 (1971):5353A-54A.

5 DOBRÉE, BONAMY. "Etherege." In Restoration Comedy, 1660-1720. London: Oxford University Press, pp. 58-77.
Reprint of 1924.B2.

6 KAUL, A. N. "The Inverted Abstractions of Restoration Comedy." In The Action of English Comedy: Studies in the Encounter of Abstraction and Experience from Shakespeare to Shaw. New Haven: Yale University Press, pp. 90-130.
Despite Kaul's misgivings about Restoration drama because of "its lack of dramatic quality," he, nevertheless, presents a challenging discussion of The Man of Mode, "perhaps the most brilliant and ruthless of Restoration comedies."

7 KREUTZ, IRVING. "Who's Holding the Mirror?" Comparative Drama 4:79-88.
Restoration drama makes no demands on one to accept any morals: the audience must make of these morals what they will, and must decide whether or not Dorimant is a knave. Thus we hold the mirror, the playwright does not. The "comedy of manners presents the world not as it is but as it appears to be."

8 MATALENE, HENRY WILLIAM, III. "A Conjecture Concerning Dramatic Presentation: With New Readings of Etherege's The Man of Mode and Cibber's The Careless Husband." Dissertation, University of Pennsylvania, 312 pp.
Working from post-Kantian epistemology and perceptual psychology, Matalene re-examines "plot" and "character," as basic terms of dramatic criticism; he then applies his findings to Cibber's sentimental comedy and to Etherege's comedy of manners. DAI, 31 (1970):2885A.

9 MUIR, KENNETH. "Sir George Etherege." In The Comedy of Manners.
London: Hutchinson, pp. 28-40.
Finds the plot of Love in a Tub "a muddle," and the lan-
guage "mostly crude and flat," but praises the character of
Sir Frederick Frollick. In She Wou'd if She Cou'd, Lady
Cockwood is a well-drawn character, but the four lovers are
the play's greatest success. In contrast to Fujimura (1952.
B1), Muir thinks Dorimant is not being held up as the perfect
courtier; and while Harriet may have tamed him, "we are left
in doubt as to whether she will not regret the bargain."

10 PERSSON, AGNES VALKAY. "Comic Character in Restoration Drama."
Dissertation, University of Colorado, 292 pp.
Based on the idea that a comic character is ignorant.
This thesis is then applied to several Restoration plays,
including some by Etherege. DAI, 31 (1971):3517A. See book,
1975.B8.

1971

A BOOKS

1 ETHEREGE, GEORGE. The Dramatic Works. 2 vols. Percy Reprints,
no. 6. Edited with introduction and notes by H. F. B. Brett-
Smith. St. Clair Shores, Mich.: Scholarly Press, cviii +
325 pp.
Reprint of 1927.A1.

2 _____. The Letterbook. Edited by Sybil Rosenfeld. New York:
Benjamin Blom, 441 pp.
Reprint of 1928.A1.

B SHORTER WRITINGS

1 BARNARD, JOHN. "Drama from the Restoration till 1710." In
English Drama to 1710. Edited by Christopher Ricks. London:
Barrie and Jenkins, pp. 375-411.
Mentions the "hybrid nature" of Love in a Tub and comments
on the middle-class ethos and city-country division in She
Wou'd if She Cou'd. Sees in The Man of Mode exploratory and
skeptical elements (i.e., Sir Fopling is the comic counterpart
of Dorimant), while raising the question: "how far do we [the
audience] identify with Dorimant?"

2 BENTLEY, THOMAS. "Money: God and King; Economic Aspects of
Restoration Comedy.: Dissertation, University of Newfoundland,
436 pp.
Prosperous merchants become the target of satire in Restoration comedy, yet--ironically--the gentleman must have

money. Consequently, "procedures of the market place are used in assessing all human relationships." <u>DAI</u>, 34 (1974):7181A.

3 LANGBAINE, GERARD. <u>Momus Triumphans: or the Plagiaries of the English Stage. . . .</u> London: N[icholas] C[ox], sold by Sam. Holford; Augustan Reprint Society, no. 150. Edited, with introduction by D. S. Rodes. Los Angeles: W. A. Clark Memorial Library, xiv + 32 pp.
     Reprint of 1688.B1; see also 1688.B2.

4 LOVE, HAROLD, ed. <u>Poeta de Tristibus</u>. London: n.p.; Augustan Reprint Society, no. 149. Los Angeles: W. A. Clark Memorial Library, xiv + 40 pp.
     Reprint of text discussed by Love in 1968.B3.

5 MARVELL, ANDREW. <u>Poems and Letters</u>. 3d ed. Edited by H. M. Margoliouth. Revised by P. Legouis and E. E. Duncan-Jones. Oxford: Clarendon Press, pp. 344-46.
     Letter no. 35 to Sir Edward Harley at Brampton Castle remarks on the Epsom escapade in which Etherege was involved with Rochester. See 1878.B2.

6 McCOLLOM, WILLIAM G. <u>The Divine Average: A View of Comedy</u>. Cleveland: Press of Case-Western Reserve University, 231 pp., see especially pp. 107-108.
     Maintains that Dorimant's speech patterns in <u>The Man of Mode</u>, the only play of Etherege's cited, sets him apart as an ideal rather than an average character. Language distinguishes the wit from the would-be wit, the fop, or the fool.

7 PRICE, STANLEY. "Aldwych: <u>Man of Mode</u>." <u>Plays and Players</u> 19 (November):38-41.
     Review of the Royal Shakespeare Company production of <u>The Man of Mode</u>, including photos. Price calls the drama "good entertainment," but the production is "stylistically at sea." Directed by Terry Hands, the cast included Alan Howard as Dorimant, Julian Glover as Medley, John Wood as Sir Fopling, Helen Mirren as Harriet, Vivien Merchant as Loveit, and Brenda Bruce as Lady Townley. See 1971.B11.

8 SCHNEIDER, BEN ROSS, JR. <u>The Ethos of Restoration Comedy</u>. Urbana, Ill.: University of Illinois Press. ix + 203 pp., passim.
     Catalogues various "type" characters in eighty-three comedies from 1660-1730. Concludes that satire implies some moral standard. Then treats several ethical norms, including generosity, bravery, straightforwardness, and love.

9 SMITH, JOHN HARRINGTON. <u>The Gay Couple in Restoration Comedy</u>. New York: Octagon, xi + 252 pp.
      Reprint of 1948.B3.

10 WAITH, EUGENE M. <u>Ideas of Greatness: Heroic Drama in England</u>. New York: Barnes and Noble, xii + 292 pp.
      Of Etherege's three plays, Waith notes only the heroic love plot in <u>Love in a Tub</u>, where "noble characters readily fall into rhymed couplets in their discussion of 'excess of Virtue' or 'some extream of Honour, or of Love' (II.ii)."

11 WATERHOUSE, R. "A Case of Restoration: Terry Hands and Timothy O'Brien Talk to Robert Waterhouse." <u>Plays and Players</u> 19 (November):14-16, 84.
      An interview with Hands, the director, and O'Brien, the designer, of the Royal Shakespeare Company production of <u>The Man of Mode</u>. Hands comments on his division of characters "into artificial and natural" groupings; and O'Brien explains why he used colorful costumes against a plain backdrop, but a more modern setting. For a review of this production, see 1971.B7.

<u>1972</u>

A BOOKS

1 ETHEREGE, GEORGE. <u>She Wou'd if She Cou'd</u>. Edited with an Intro-duction by Charlene M. Taylor. Regents Restoration Drama Series. Lincoln: University of Nebraska Press. xxix + 132 pp.
      Argues that Restoration comedy gains its distinctive nature from a fusion of social, romantic, artificial, and intellectual strains, and that <u>She Wou'd if She Cou'd</u> is the first Restora-tion comedy to combine these four elements. Each of the four is discussed as it appears in various parts of the play.

B SHORTER WRITINGS

1 BATESON, F. W. "Second Thoughts: L. C. Knights and Restoration Comedy." In <u>Essays in Critical Dissent</u>. Totwa, N. J.: Rowan and Littlefield, pp. 117-27.
      Reprint of 1957.B2, with a few revisions.

2 BEAR, ANDREW. "Restoration Comedy and the Provok'd Critic." In <u>Restoration Literature: Critical Approaches</u>. Edited by Harold Love. London: Methuen; New York: Barnes and Noble, pp. 1-26.
      Considers the critical controversies of "moralistic

1972

criticism versus literary judgment." Phase One (the eighteenth century) attacked the plays on moral grounds. Phase
Two (the nineteenth century) found defenders in Lamb (1822.B1)
and Hazlitt (1819.B1), who said that immorality had nothing to
do with literary quality. Macaulay (1841.B1), on the other
hand, carried the torch of Victorian morality. Phase Three
becomes more complex in the twentieth century: L. C. Knights
(1937.B1) attacks the plays where Lamb chose to defend them,
(i.e., attacks their literary quality). Bear then carefully
dismantles Knights's arguments and deals coherently with each
point.

3 DAVIES, PAUL C. "Restoration Liberalism." Essays in Criticism
   22:226-38.
      Cites, among other Restoration authors, Etherege, whose
   letters show that the poet (as diplomat) was sympathetic
   towards authoritarian rule, whereas in his private and personal
   life Etherege was much more liberal.

*4 DEEPAK, K. "The Strain of the Sentimental in Restoration and
   Eighteenth-Century Comedy." Dissertation, Australian National.
      In McNamee.

5 DEITZ, JONATHAN ERIC. "The Design of Plot: The New Directions
   in Plot Resolution of Late Restoration Satiric Comedy." Dissertation, University of Pennsylvania, 242 pp.
      Examines differences in the ironic plot structure of early
   Restoration comedy--by Dryden, Wycherley, and Etherege--in
   order to show how it differs from satiric plot structure later
   in the century in plays by Vanbrugh, Congreve, and Farquhar.
   DAI, 33(1973):3640A.

6 HAWKINS, HARRIET. "'Vice under Character of Advantage':
   Dramatic and Social Success in The Man of Mode." In
   Likenesses of Truth in Elizabethan and Restoration Drama.
   Oxford: Clarendon Press, pp. 79-97.
      Reacting against the moralistic interpretations of Under-
   wood (1957.A1), Powell (1965.B5), and Sutherland (1969.B10),
   Hawkins sees the merging of the techniques of Ovid's Art of
   Love with the art of theatre; both require acting. And it is
   those who act best that are the most successful in comic
   drama. If we get instruction from the play, it is not moral
   but social, and we learn "about masks people wear, and about
   the way people play the game of love."

7 HUME, ROBERT D. "Diversity and Development in Restoration Comedy,
   1660-1679." Eighteenth-Century Studies 5:365-97.
      Notes that Love in a Tub combines the four elements that

were popular in 1664 into four plots: 1) the humorous court-
ship of Sir Frederick Frollick and Widow Rich, 2) love and
honor intrigues, 3) Nicholas Cully duped, and 4) "low" comedy
of Dufoy as a satire against the French. Argues against the
evolutionary view that She Wou'd if She Cou'd (1668) launched
the "comedy of manners." Concludes "early Restoration comedy
[must be] considered as comprising a variety of types," but we
must also "see the influence of changing audience taste."

8 _____. "Reading and Misreading The Man of Mode." Criticism 14:
       1-11.
       In The Man of Mode, audience response is extremely impor-
tant as to our judgment of the characters. After tracing the
varied criticisms of The Man of Mode, Hume reads the play as
a "delightful satiric entertainment," which is not necessarily
profound. Ultimately, he sides with Davies's claim (1969.B2)
that The Man of Mode "is an uncompromisingly tough and realistic play," and with Powell (1965.B5) that we are "left
floating between laughter and indignation."

9 JORDAN, ROBERT. "The Extravagant Rake in Restoration Comedy."
      In Restoration Literature. Edited by Harold Love. London:
      Methuen, pp. 69-90.
       Contrasts the extravagant rake with the gentleman rake;
both types emerge between 1663-68. The characteristics of the
extravagant rake are wildness in language and action, frivoli-
ty, impulsiveness, and imprudence; he is regarded as eccentric
and unique. While he is comic, he is not a fool because of
his self-awareness. Dorimant is noted for his control, his
smooth social manner, and his cultivated charm. He is the
gentleman rake, who has judgmental traits that are lacking in
the extravagant rake, who is always on holiday, "filling a
carnival role."

10 KISHI, TETSUO. "George Etherege and the Destiny of Restoration
      Comedy." In English Criticism in Japan. Edited by Earl Miner.
      Tokyo: University of Tokyo Press, pp. 156-69.
       Discusses the several plots of Love in a Tub--four varia-
tions of "honourable heroic actions." Among the parallels and
contrasts mentioned are Sir Frederick's parody of Lord Bevill's
heroic verse, the tub and bier scenes, the twin duels, and the
role reversals (Palmer imitates Lord Bevill, Grace acts Mrs.
Rich, and Sir Nicholas pretends to be a gallant like Sir
Frederick). What looks like disunity is an ambivalent attitude on the part of the author toward heroic virtue, and "this
ambivalence is at the root of the aesthetics of Restoration
comedy." Translated from Japanese version (1968.B10) and
slightly revised.

1972

11 LOFTIS, JOHN. "The Limits of Historical Veracity in Neoclassic
    Drama." In England in the Restoration and Early Eighteenth
    Century. Edited by H. T. Swendenberg, Jr. Berkeley: Univer-
    sity of California Press, pp. 27-50.
        "What kind of historical information, if any, can we ex-
    pect the drama to yield?" is the question Loftis considers in
    the light of recent social and demographic history. Asks if
    The Man of Mode is an accurate picture of upper-class life,
    and concludes that although plays are not reliable guides,
    they reveal, as statistics cannot, "the emotional dimension of
    a sociological fact."

12 OLSHEN, BARRY NEIL. "The Reception of Restoration Comedy of
    Manners in Nineteenth-Century England: An Account of
    Wycherley, Congreve, Vanbrugh, and Farquhar on the Stage and
    in the Study." Dissertation, University of Toronto.
        Notes that "Etherege was extinct" on the nineteenth cen-
    tury stage. DAI, 34 (1974):5374A-75A.

13 RODWAY, ALLAN. "Restoration Comedy Re-examined." Renaissance
    and Modern Studies 16:37-60.
        Treats the exploration of ideas by dramatic characters
    probing moral issues, because the dualism of the characters
    gives them the ability to deal with society's norms. They
    react against Puritan dogma in order to explore and test a
    "rational morality." Because Etherege himself withholds
    judgment, The Man of Mode is "a genuine experimental comedy in
    which the author takes no side. The play is thus closer to a
    divertissement than a moralistic comedy: the whole encourages
    laughter neither with, nor at, but about."

1973

A BOOKS

1 ETHEREGE, GEORGE. The Man of Mode; or, Sir Fopling Flutter.
    Edited by John Conaghan. Fountainwell Drama Series, no. 23.
    Edinburgh: Oliver and Boyd, 135 pp.
        Critical introduction compares The Man of Mode with contem-
    porary Restoration comedies. Points out a "series of character
    contrasts which help to define Dorimant and limit his role:
    with Medley, with Young Bellair, and especially with Sir
    Fopling."

2 _____. The Man of Mode; or, Sir Fopling Flutter. In Restoration
    and Eighteenth-Century Comedy. Edited by Scott McMillin. New
    York: Norton, pp. 79-151.
        Reprint of 1676 quarto. Includes reprints of critical

essays: 1973.B1, B3, B6, B7, B11, B12, B14.

3 _____. The Man of Mode; or, Sir Fopling Flutter. In Three Restoration Comedies. Edited by Gamini Salgado, Harmondsworth,
Middlesex: Penguin, pp. 28-33, 43-146.
        Reprint of 1968.A2.

4 _____. She Wou'd if She Cou'd. Edited with an Introduction by
Charlene M. Taylor. Regents Restoration Drama Series.
Lincoln: University of Nebraska Press; London: Edward Arnold,
xxix + 132 pp.
        Reprint of 1972.A1.

B SHORTER WRITINGS

1 DENNIS, JOHN. "A Defence of Sir Fopling Flutter." In Restoration
and Eighteenth-Century Comedy. Edited by Scott McMillin. New
York: Norton, pp. 429-32.
        Reprint of 1722.B1.

2 FERRELL, DAVID MICHAEL. "The Structural Functions of Rake
Characters in Restoration Comedy." Dissertation, University
of Missouri at Columbia, 193 pp.
        Study of eight rake characters in the comedies of Etherege,
Wycherley, and Congreve. Labels Sir Frederick (Love in a Tub)
and Courtall (She Wou'd if She Cou'd) as "rakes gaining ad-
mittance into the social world," whereas Dorimant is a mature
rake (i.e., he is already accepted into the social milieu,
where he uses "its follies and pretenses to suit" himself).
DAI, 35 (1974):1281A.

3 FUJIMURA, THOMAS H. "[The Man of Mode as a Comedy of Wit]."
In Restoration and Eighteenth-Century Comedy. Edited by
Scott McMillin, pp. 504-13.
        Reprint of 1952.B1, pp. 104-16.

4 HAMMOND, ANTHONY. "'Beau' Hewyt and John Crowne." Notes and
Queries 218:466-67.
        Corrects Sherbo (1949.B4) in a reference to Crowne's
dedicatee in the tragedy of Darius: it is an Irish knight
Sir George Hewyt, not Beau Hewyt.

5 HUME, ROBERT D. "Theory of Comedy in the Restoration." Modern
Philology 70:302-18.
        There is no neat, tidy theory that will apply to all comedy
of the later seventeenth century. Hume uses the Steele-Dennis
clash over The Man of Mode (see 1711.B4 and 1722.B1) to show
the comic theories of "example" and of "ridicule." The many

1973

modes of comedy should make the reader "beware of all-
inclusive statements about this drama."

6 KNIGHTS, L. C. "Restoration Comedy: The Reality and the Myth."
In <u>Restoration and Eighteenth-Century Comedy</u>. Edited by Scott
McMillin. New York: Norton, pp. 494-504.
Reprint of 1937.B1.

7 LAMB, CHARLES. "On the Artificial Comedy of the Last Century."
In <u>Restoration and Eighteenth-Century Comedy</u>. Edited by Scott
McMillin. Norton, pp. 479-84.
Reprint of 1822.B1.

8 LANGHANS, EDWARD A. "New Restoration Manuscript Casts." <u>Theatre
Notebook</u> 27:149-56.
Mentions <u>The Lacedemonian Mercury</u> report of 7 March 1692,
and notes a revival of <u>The Man of Mode</u> because of the 1693
printing. (See 1692.B1 and 1693.A2.) The last revival of <u>The
Man of Mode</u> had been in 1684, as confirmed by a cast list in
the Harvard Theatre collection. Langhans suggests that the
revival took place between 7 March 1692 and December 1692,
the death of Anthony Leigh, who is mentioned in the cast list.

9 LEWIS, MINEKO S. "Humor Characterization in Restoration Comedy,
1660-1700." Dissertation, University of Tennessee.
Sees "a common tradition" of humor characterization, bind-
ing "the comedies of Shadwell, Dryden, and Wycherley with
those of Etherege and Congreve." <u>DAI</u>, 34 (1973):1247A.

10 LIGHTFOOT, JOHN EWELL, JR. "The Treatment of Women in Restoration Comedy of Manners." Dissertation, Texas Technological
University, 206 pp.
Etherege, Wycherley, and Congreve "were willing to grant
women more intellectual and social freedom than was available
to the sex at large in England from 1660-1700." Detailed
attention given to Ariana and Gatty in <u>She Wou'd if She Cou'd</u>
and to Harriet in <u>The Man of Mode</u>. <u>DAI</u>, 34 (1974):5918A.

11 PALMER, JOHN. "[The Comedy of Manners]." In <u>Restoration and
Eighteenth-Century Comedies</u>. Edited by Scott McMillin. New
York: Norton, pp. 484-89.
Reprint of 1913.B3, pp. 288-97.

12 POWELL, JOCELYN. "George Etherege and the Form of a Comedy."
In <u>Restoration and Eighteenth-Century Comedies</u>. New York:
Norton, pp. 513-20.
Reprint of 1965.B5.

13 RUBIN, BARBARA L. "'Anti-Husbandry' and Self-Creation: A
    Comparison of Restoration Rake and Baudelaire's Dandy."
    Texas Studies in Language and Literature, 14:583-92.
        Relates Restoration rakes (especially Dorimant) to "dandies
    of the late nineteenth century." The similarities exist be-
    cause both the rake and the dandy "refuse to join the social
    order through marriage."

14 STEELE, RICHARD. "Spectator, No. 65 of 15 May 1711." In Restora-
    tion and Eighteenth-Century Comedies. Edited by Scott
    McMillin. New York: Norton, pp. 420-22.
        Reprint of 1711.B4.

1974

A BOOKS

1 ETHEREGE, SIR GEORGE. Letters. Edited by Frederick Bracher.
    Berkeley: University of California Press, xxv + 324 pp.
        Reprints the most important letters of Etherege from three
    main sources--the Letterbook (1928.A1), the Middleton papers
    (1934.B5), and the second Letterbook (at Harvard--1952.B4),
    plus several from a variety of locations. See 1975.B6 for an
    .important review.

2 ETHEREGE, GEORGE. The Man of Mode; or, Sir Fopling Flutter. In
    Restoration Comedy. 4 vols. Edited by A. Norman Jeffares.
    London: Folio Society; Totowa, N. J.: Rowman and Littlefield,
    1:517-624.
        Reprints of first edition, 1676.A1, with brief introduction
    and textual notes.

3 _____. She Wou'd if She Cou'd. In Restoration Comedy. 4 vols.
    Edited by A. Norman Jeffares. London: Folio Society; Totowa,
    N.J.: Rowman and Littlefield, 1:217-305.
        Reprint of first edition, 1668.A1, with brief introduction
    and textual notes.

4 McCAMIC, FRANCES SMITH. Sir George Etherege: A Study in Restora-
    tion Comedy (1660-1680). Folcraft, Pa.: Folcraft Library
    Editions, 95 pp.
        Reprint of 1931.A3.

B SHORTER WRITINGS

1 BRUCE, DONALD. Topics of Restoration Comedy. London: Gollancz,
    pp. 122-25, passim.
        Considers Etherege's plays in the tradition of Middleton's

101

1974

comedies. "Epicureanism," one of the topics, describes the
life of Dorimant exactly; in fact, Dorimant is the "Petronian
Epicure." Sees four parts of his love-chase in The Man of
Mode: vainglory, power over others, a taste for variety, and
a distaste for yet curiousity about passion. Harriet is "the
earliest of Suffragettes."

2 ELLEHAUGE, MARTIN. English Restoration Drama: Its Relation to
Past English and Past and Contemporary French Drama. From
Jonson via Molière to Congreve. Folcraft, Pa.: Folcraft
Library Editions, passim.
Reprint of 1933.B1.

3 FLATTERY, BRUCE. "Renaissance and Restoration Perspectives on
the Experience of Comedy." Dissertation, University of
Toronto.
Examines audience response to the image of society in
seventeenth-century comedy, including Etherege. Concludes
that Restoration comedy has a limited world view; it provides
only "mere diversion and social criticism." DAI, 38 (1977):
3479A.

4 HANSON, JOHN H. "The Language of Eros in Restoration Comedy."
Dissertation, State University of New York-Buffalo.
Takes up psychoanalytical and philosophical approaches in
plays of Etherege, Wycherley, and Congreve. Concludes that in
all three playwrights there is a collective psychological
experience of society and ideology. Chapter on Etherege en-
titled "Etherege and Gold's Guardian Angels." DAI, 35 (1975):
4429A.

5 HARTMAN, JAY HARRY. "A Stylistic Study of the Comedies of Etherege, Wycherley, and Congreve." Dissertation, Lehigh University,
395 pp.
Detects possible influence of Etherege on Wycherley, and
of both playwrights on Congreve. DAI, 35 (1974):2223A.

6 MINER, EARL R. The Restoration Mode from Milton to Dryden.
Princeton: Princeton University Press, pp. 368-72, 376-80.
Some remarks on Love in a Tub, but a longer discussion on
Etherege's poetic contribution to such conventions as the
imperfect enjoyment poem (see also 1963.B4), the frolic or
ramble poem, and the epistolary poem. Finds that the complex-
ity of Etherege's character "makes him difficult to puzzle
out."

7 STUPNIKOV, IGOR. "Dzhordzh Eteridzh, 1634-1691, i ego p'eas
'Komicheskoe Mshchenie'" [George Etherege, 1634-1691, and his

play "The Comical Revenge."]. <u>Nauchnge koklady vysshei shkoly.</u>
<u>Filologicheskie nauki.</u> [<u>Philological Sciences</u>] (Moscow) 5,
no. 83:25-35.
    In Russian.

<u>1975</u>

A BOOKS

*1 ETHEREGE, GEORGE. <u>Komicheskoe Mshchenie</u> [<u>The Comical Revenge</u>].
Translated, with introduction by Igor Stupnikov. Moscow:
Iskusstvo, 127 pp.
    In Russian. Listed <u>MHRA Annual Bibliography</u>.

2 ____. <u>The Man of Mode; or, Sir Fopling Flutter</u>. In <u>British</u>
<u>Dramatists from Dryden to Sheridan</u>. Edited by George H.
Nettleton and Arthur E. Case. Revised by George W. Stone, Jr.
Carbondale: Southern Illinois University Press, pp. 153-95.
    Reprint of 1939.A1 text, with revised notes and biblio-
graphy by Stone, 1969.A1.

3 ____. <u>The Works of Sir George Etherege: Plays and Poems</u>.
Edited by A. W. Verity. Norwood, Pa.: Norwood Editions, xxxi
+ 408 pp.
    Reprint of 1888.A1.

B SHORTER WRITINGS

1 BARNARD, JOHN. "Etherege, Shadwell, Wycherley, Congreve, Vanbrugh,
and Farquhar." In <u>English Drama (excluding Shakespeare):</u>
<u>Select Bibliographical Guides</u>. Edited by Stanley Wells.
London: Oxford University Press, pp. 173-98.
    Bibliographical essay. Takes up general works on the
comedies of the writers in the title, then deals with each
individual writer.

2 BRATTON, CLINTON WOODROW. "The Use of Marriage in the Comedies
of Etherege, Wycherley, Dryden, and Congreve." Dissertation,
University of Colorado, 174 pp.
    Considers the question of morality in the comedies of the
playwrights in the title. Finds in Etherege that the libertine's pleasures are halted by the non-libertine heroine.
When the libertine is thus forced to re-examine his views, he
renounces his libertinism. <u>DAI</u>, 36 (1976):7431A-32A.

3 BROWN, HAROLD CLIFFORD, JR. "Etherege and the Comic Shallowness."
<u>Texas Studies in Language and Literature</u> 16:675-90.
    "Attempt[s] to define the heroes' shallowness, in philo-

1975

sophy [Nietzsche] and in cultural schizophrenia [Karen
Horner]." The libertine protagonists of Etherege's plays all
suffer from neuroses; this gives them a "resigned shallowness."

4 GRATZ, DAVID KENNETH. "Emotion, Modes of Expression and Effects
on Plot in Selected Comedies: 1670-1780." Dissertation,
Syracuse University, 265 pp.
Studies how emotions--overt or covert--effect the plots of
various plays from Etherege to Sheridan. Only The Man of Mode
is treated. DAI, 36 (1976):6702A.

5 HUSEBOE, ARTHUR. "The Mother of Sir George Etherege." Notes and
Queries 220:262-64.
New information on the playwright's mother (born, 1622;
died, 1699) and family. Huseboe offers a suggestion that
Etherege may have turned to writing plays to support his
widowed mother after the death of her second husband in 1662.

6 _____. "Review of The Letters of Sir George Etherege." Modern
Philology 73:194-200.
Lengthy and helpful review of 1974.A1.

7 McDONALD, MARGARET LAMB. "The Independent Woman in the Restoration Comedy of Manners." Dissertation, University of Colorado.
262 pp.
Develops three basic characteristics for the independent
Restoration heroine--wit and intelligence, will to power, and
heightened awareness. Harriet "can balance fancy with judgment,
handle the play of ideas as well as a play on words, and manage
to cope with the repressive limitations of [this society]."
DAI, 36 (1975):2850-51A. See book, 1976.B6.

8 PERSSON, AGNES VALKAY. Comic Characters in Restoration Drama.
De Proprietatibus Litterarum Series Practica, no. 99. The
Hague: Mouton, 151 pp., passim.
Lumps assorted comic characters into various categories of
ignorance and awareness. Proofreading errors. See Disserta-
tion, 1970.B10.

9 RODWAY, ALLAN. "Etherege, Wycherley, Congreve, Farquhar." In
English Comedy: Its Role and Nature from Chaucer to the
Present Day. London: Chatto and Windus, pp. 124-43, see
especially pp. 127-32.
Etherege in The Man of Mode provides no standard of values,
so tone and style matter more than the content of the imagery.
Explores the theme of emotion endangering freedom, and
concludes that the whole of the rather cynical comedy "encour-
ages laughter neither with, nor at, but about." Slightly

revised from an earlier essay (1972.B13).

10 TULLY, VELMA ANITA. "Innocence and Experience as Structural
   Comic Values in Selected Plays of the Restoration and Eighteenth Century." Dissertation, University of Arkansas.
      The Man of Mode (among other comedies) is analyzed for
   "comic uses of innocence and experience." DAI, 36 (1975):
   3666A.

1976

A BOOKS

1 ETHEREGE, GEORGE. The Man of Mode; or, Sir Fopling Flutter. In
   Three Restoration Comedies. Edited with introduction by
   Gamini Salgado. Harmondsworth, Middlesex: Penguin, pp. 28-33,
   43-146.
      Reprint of 1968.A2.

2 RIGAUD, NADIA J. "George Etherege: Dramaturge de la Restauration
   Anglaise." Dissertation, Sorbonne, Paris, 944 pp. (629 pp. of
   text, 315 pp. of notes, bibliography, and appendices).
      Background of Sir George Etherege and his age, followed
   by an analysis of each comedy. Extensive treatment of the
   characters--heroes, heroines, fools, sages; passions; structures; and language.

B SHORTER WRITINGS

1 BORKAT, ROBERTA F. S. "Vows, Prayers, and Dice: Comic Values
   in The Man of Mode." University of Dayton Review 12:121-31.
      Demonstrates that individual passion (through the meta-
   phors of religion) and art (through the metaphors of gaming)
   combine as possible values in the world of the play. In
   contrast, social rank, as espoused by Old Bellair and Lady
   Woodvil, becomes valueless.

2 FORD, DAN. "'Smelling as one Does': A Comment on Time in The
   Man of Mode." Papers of the Arkansas Philological Association
   2, no. iii:22-28.
      Deals with Dorimant's "attempt to establish a pleasurable
   present in the midst of rapid change," by Etherege's keeping
   "the audience aware of natural temporal succession." Argues
   that Dorimant's "multiple existence" gives way to single love
   for Harriet; yet "we are not certain of the stability of any
   relationship as the play ends."

3 HUME, ROBERT D. The Development of English Drama in the late

1976

Seventeenth Century. Oxford: Clarendon Press, pp. 86-97,
245-46, 265-67, passim.
Notes, in Love in a Tub, the four plots and post-Restora-
tion sources: 1) love-honor plot (Tuke), 2) Sir Frederick and
widow Rich plot (Sir Robert Howard, The Committee; Edward
Howard, The English Mounsieur), 3) the gulling of Cully (E.
Howard, ibid., J. Wilson, The Cheats, Dryden The Wild Gallant), and Dufoy's tub farce (E. Howard, ibid.). In She Wou'd
if She Cou'd, Hume cites two principal plots: 1) Lady Cockwood and her drive for extra-marital sex, 2) the witty young
lovers. These plots exhibit character and refined language.
While She Wou'd if She Cou'd is unique, it does not really
start a new trend. Etherege is not the norm for his time,
because his social focus and his emphasis on character is too
narrow. Thus, the comedy in the latter half of the century
does not follow Etherege's lead. His discussion of The Man of
Mode virtually repeats his earlier essay (1972.B7) with no
major modifications.

4 LINK, FREDERICK M. English Drama, 1660-1800. A Guide to Information Sources, no. 9. Detroit, Michigan: Gale Research, pp.
168-71.
Bibliographical essay on criticism of Etherege's work.

5 MARTIN, LESLIE H. "Past and Parody in The Man of Mode." Studies
in English Literature 16:363-76.
Through an understanding of Loveit's temperament and
values, the audience can see the parody of heroic drama; the
"freedoms of the present" triumph over the hypocritical, joy-
less past.

6 McDONALD, MARGARET LAMB. The Independent Woman in the Restoration Comedy of Manners. Salzburg Studies: Poetic Drama and
Poetic Theory, no. 32. Salzburg Institut für Englische Sprache
und Literatur. Salzburg: Universität Salzburg, pp. 63-66,
88-96, 222-25, passim.
Shows that heroines of Restoration comedy display self-
awareness, intelligence, wit, and self-determination. These
heroines have read Hobbes and understand him as well (if not
better than) the heroes. Considers Dryden's Florimell, in
Secret Love, as the prototype of Etherege's Harriet. See
Dissertation, 1975.B7.

7 MLA Seminar, no. 383. 28 December 1976 on the tercentenary of
The Man of Mode. Co-chairmen: A. D. Kaufmann and David Mann.
Panel: Shirley Strum Kenny, Earl Miner, Eugene Waith, and
Albert Wertheim.
For a précis of the papers, see Restoration 1 (1977):3.

1977

8 MONROE, RUTH ELLA. "Conflict and Compromise: A Study of
   Conflict Resolution in Etherege, Congreve, and Restoration
   Politics." Dissertation, University of Minnesota, 524 pp.
       Plays by Etherege and Congreve reflect political behavior
   in a negotiated resolution by compromise. Chapters 3 to 5
   treat the conflicts in Etherege's comedies, the political
   events contemporary with the plays, and the parallel transac-
   tions on stage and in politics. The political game theory,
   important in both playwrights, "might by used as a basic
   underlying concept in production." DAI, 37 (1976):3274A.

9 SCOUTEN, ARTHUR H. "Sir George Etherege." In The Revels History
   of Drama in England, 1660-1750. Vol. 5. General editor, T.
   W. Craik. London: Methuen, pp. 178-86.
       The plots of Love in a Tub are tightly held together by
   interwoven episode and imagery. In She Wou'd if She Cou'd,
   we see "the triumph of experience over hope." In The Man of
   Mode, "a group of self-centered people are engaged . . . in
   role playing."

*10 STUPNIKOV, IGOR. "George Etherege's She Wou'd if She Cou'd."
   Perm University Papers.
       Announced in RECTR, 14 (1975) for publication in 1976.
   Stupnikov has also proposed an edition of She Wou'd if She
   Cou'd. In Russian.

11 WILSON, JOHN HAROLD, ed. Court Satires of the Restoration.
   Columbus: Ohio State University Press, xxiii + 304 pp.
       Includes several poems, printed from manuscripts of the
   period, that mention Etherege. "Julian's Farewell to the
   Muses," for example, comments on "fluxing George" and his
   "sharp mercurial wit."

1977

A BOOKS

1 ETHEREGE, GEORGE. The Works of Sir George Etherege: Plays and
   Poems. Edited by A. W. Verity. Philadelphia: R. West,
   xxxi + 408 pp.
       Reprint of 1888.A1.

B SHORTER WRITINGS

1 BELESS, ROSEMARY JUNE. "Reflections of the Law in the Comedies
   of Etherege, Wycherley, and Congreve." Dissertation, University of Utah, 174 pp.
       Use of the law as a source of rhethorical materials and

thematic ideas, such as equity, matrimonial law, equality of
women, and dishonest attorneys in order to suggest reform of
abuses. All the plays of Etherege included. DAI, 38 (1977):
2801A.

2 CORMAN, BRIAN. "Interpreting and Misinterpreting The Man of
Mode." Papers in Language and Literature 13:35-53.
Working from the argument between Steele and Dennis (1711.
B4; 1722.B1), Corman establishes that Dorimant is a comic hero
(not Steele's exemplary Bevill), but a hero who is forced to
undergo comic punishments. The Young Bellair-Old Bellair-
Emilia triangle supports the argument of comedy, whereas the
Dorimant-Harriet-Lady Woodvil triangle is a parallel plot,
with a twist. Concludes that Dorimant's "commitment to Harriet,
while disappointing to some is not out of character."

3 HUME, ROBERT D. "Marital Discord in English Comedy from Dryden
to Fielding." Modern Philology 74:248-72.
Discusses marriage in satiric and reform comedies from
1660 to 1737: "Marital discord is inherently problem comedy."
Most marital discords rely on the appeal of inversion, such
as the Cockwoods in She Wou'd if She Cou'd: "a domineering
wife tyrannizes an ineffectual rebellious husband." The
romantic assumption that marriage is a guaranteed happy ending
is challenged by plays with a "dose of realism."

4 _____. "The Myth of the Rake in 'Restoration' Comedy." Studies
in Literary Imagination 10:25-55.
Finds, contrary to traditional views, that rakes are
"seldom anything but comic exaggerations, satiric butts, and
bedroom farce conventions." Etherege's Dorimant, however, is
a notable exception. And though The Man of Mode should not
be considered a libertine tract, Dorimant is a tough-minded
seducer of society belles. As a reformed rake, he succumbs to
love, "tamed by a woman even tougher and more self-controlled
than he."

5 KAVENIK, FRANCES MARY-MICHELE. "The Restoration Repertory
Theatre: 1659-1668." Dissertation, University of Wisconsin.
317 pp.
Explores the use of the theatrical repertory system at
the beginning of the Restoration and applies the demands of
repertory company performances to three comedies, including
Etherege's She Wou'd if She Cou'd. DAI, 38 (1977):3516A.

6 NOVAK, MAXIMILLIAN. "Margery Pinchwife's 'London Disease': Restoration Comedy in the Libertine Offensive of the 1670's."
Studies in Literary Imagination 10:1-23.

1978

Shows, through a reading of poems, pamphlets, and plays
of the 1670s, that the country stood for traditional ideas of
marriage, whereas the city supported the pleasures of the
town and sexual freedom. By the time The Man of Mode was
produced, "the quarrel had lost its edge and was blending into
what was to become . . . only a settled contempt for the nar-
rowness of country life."

7 PIRAGES, PHILIP JOE. "The Formative Years of Restoration Comedy."
  Dissertation, University of Michigan.
      Studies the plays of the 1660s, concluding that there is
  a variety in the experimentation of the playwrights. "When
  successful," the new plays, "brought imitations and inspired
  trends." DAI, 38 (1978):6748A.

8 RAY, JIMMIE KAREN COUCH. "The Velvet Vizard: The Ethic of Dissimulation in Restoration Comedy." Dissertation, University
  of Texas at Austin, 286 pp.
      A study of the dissimulation, the motives, and the re-
  sponses in the plays of Etherege, Wycherley, and Congreve.
  Understanding this background, the audience can grasp the
  "value system of Restoration comedy." DAI, 38 (1977):7348A.

9 VIETH, DAVID M. "Divided Consciousness: The Trauma and Triumph
  of Restoration Culture." Tennessee Studies in Literature 22:
  46-62.
      Classifies The Man of Mode as representing a "many-sided
  awareness" on the part of Etherege, whose characters represent
  a variety of attitudes in a number of "relativistic situations."

10 YOUNG, DOUGLAS MORTON. "The Virtuous Women in the Restoration
   Play-World: The Concept of Marriage and the Social Status of
   Women in the Comedies of Etherege, Wycherley, and Congreve."
   Dissertation, Florida State University, 439 pp.
       All three playwrights develop alternative positions re-
   garding women to those traditionally held. Harriet has some
   qualities of both Widow Rich and Gatty, "his two underdeveloped
   ladies of virtue in his earlier plays, but he has endowed
   Harriet with greater maturity and intellectual ability." DAI,
   38 (1979):5133A.

1978

A BOOKS

1 ETHEREGE, GEORGE. The Man of Mode; or, Sir Fopling Flutter. In
  Twenty-Three Plays: An Introductory Anthology. Edited by
  Otto Reinert and Peter Arnott. Boston: Little, Brown, pp.

1978

335-414.
Provides a discussion following the play, emphasizing sex comedy and duality in the major characters.

B SHORTER WRITINGS

1 DANCHIN, PIERRE. The Prologues and Epilogues of the Restoration (1660-1700): A Tentative Check-List. Nancy: L'Université de Nancy II, x + 215 pp.
A checklist of Prologues and Epilogues from the 1659-60 theatrical season to December 1700. Notes those of Love in a Tub and The Man of Mode but has found none for She Wou'd if She Cou'd. Also cites Etherege's Prologue to the opening of the Duke's New Playhouse, 9 November 1671. A revised checklist to follow this "tentative" one.

*2 GAGEN, JEAN E. "The Comic Design of Etherege's The Comical Revenge." Paper delivered at Midwestern American Society of Eighteenth-Century Studies, 17 November 1978 in Restoration Drama section, University of Kansas.

3 HUSEBOE, ARTHUR R. "Etherege's She Would if She Could, I.i.134." In Studies in English and American Literature. Edited by John L. Cutler and Lawrence S. Thompson. American Notes and Queries Supplement, Vol. 1. Troy, N. Y.: Whitson Publishing, pp. 133-35.
Argues that "feeing in the cause" is the correct reading for Sir Oliver's remark to Courtall (not "feeling in the cause").

4 JANTZ, URSULA. Targets of Satire in the Comedies of Etherege, Wycherley, and Congreve. Salzburg Studies in English Literature, Poetic Drama and Poetic Theory, no. 42. Institut für Englische Sprache und Literatur. Salzburg: Universität Salzburg, 242 pp.
"Targets" include hypocrisy, affectation, and materialism in Part 1, and subjects (marriage, the court, etc.) and types of people (lawyers, clergy, etc.) in Part 2. Uses examples from all of Etherege's plays.

5 LEON, EDELMA de. "The Dramatic Function of Bawdy in the Plays of George Etherege." Papers of the Arkansas Philological Association 4, no. ii:45-49.
Bawdy functions three ways in Etherege's comedies: 1) as a comic device, 2) as a device of characterization, and 3) as an ironic device. Concludes that bawdy in Love in a Tub is salaciously comic; in She Wou'd if She Cou'd, it "serves to delineate character"; and in The Man of Mode, it "is an integral part of the dramatic structure."

1979

6 VAN DER WEELE, STEVEN JOHN. The Critical Reputation of Restoration Comedy in Modern Times up to 1950. 2 vols. Salzburg
Studies in English Literature, Poetic Drama and Poetic Theory,
no. 36. Institut für Englische Sprache und Literatur.
Salzburg: Universität Salzburg, 637 pp. See especially pp.
413-34.
   After a brief biography, Van Der Weele comments on several
critical works: 1866.B1; 1881.B2; a review of 1888.A1; 1901.
A1; 1927.A1; 1928.B1; 1931.A3; and 1952.B3. See Ph.D. Dissertation, 1955.B7.

*7 WAITH, EUGENE M. "'Give me your Hands': Reflections on the
Author's Agents in Comedy." In The Author in His Work:
Essays on a Problem in Criticism. Edited by Louis L. Martz
and Aubery Williams. New Haven: Yale University Press, pp.
197-213.
   Concludes with a lengthy discussion of The Man of Mode.
[Cited in Restoration, 2 (Fall, 1978):24.]

8 ZIMBARDO, R[OSE] A. "Imitation to Emulation: 'Imitation of
Nature' from the Restoration to the Eighteenth Century."
Restoration 2, no. ii:2-9.
   Sees four stages that "the conception 'imitation of
nature' undergoes from 1660 to 1730. Cites The Man of Mode
as being in Stage Two; "'nature' lies somewhere between
imaginative idealization and the corrupt actual."

1979

A BOOKS

1 ETHEREGE, GEORGE. The Man of Mode; or, Sir Fopling Flutter.
Edited by John Barnard. New Mermaid Series. London: Benn;
New York: Norton, xlvii + 152 pp.
   Introduction provides relevant background information,
followed by a lengthy discussion of the play. Asks: "what
attitude should the audience take toward Dorimant?" Even
characters on stage react to him in ambiguous ways. If the
audience sees the basic conflict between generations, they
can grasp the idea developed by Harriet and Dorimant (which
Mrs. Loveit or Sir Fopling cannot understand): "new freedoms
may bring more danger, but they also offer more choice and the
chance of self-determinism." Even though love is irrational
and temporary in its nature, Harriet and Dorimant are willing
to take that risk.

1979

B SHORTER WRITINGS

1 HIRST, DAVID L. Comedy of Manners. The Critical Idiom series,
no. 40. London: Methuen, pp. 17-21, passim.
Sees in The Man of Mode (the only one of Etherege's plays
discussed) the "ruthlessness of society," citing Mrs. Loveit's
outbursts "there's nothing but falsehood and impertinence in
this world," or "there's no truth in friendship neither," to
prove his case. Also notes that "the play is much concerned
with tone, style, and the dangers of sincerity."

2 HOLLAND, PETER. The Ornament of Action: Text and Performance in
Restoration Comedy. Cambridge: Cambridge University Press,
284 pp., passim.
Plays are studied in relation to their performance, including the audience, the theatres, the actors, and the text.
Treats the use of "discoveries" in The Man of Mode, showing
how they comment on Dorimant's character. Discusses the
scenery in She Wou'd if She Cou'd and argues that the locations
of action assist the audience in understanding meaning.

3 MALEK, JAMES S. "Sir George Etherege." In Great Writers of the
English Language: Dramatists. Edited by James Vinson.
London: Macmillan, pp. 198-201.
An overview of the plays. "Etherege's heroes and heroines
are always evenly matched, and because they seldom face problems imposed by the external world, happiness is achieved
when they overcome obstacles resulting from their own characters." Most of the examples from Love in a Tub and The Man
of Mode.

4 PARK, ROY. "Lamb and Restoration Comedy." Essays in Criticism
29:225-43.
Observes that Lamb's essay makes three points: 1) Restoration comedy is fun, 2) the theatre creates "dramatic il-
lusion," 3) there has been too much "realistic criteria" set
up for Restoration comedy. "Art is not life." See 1943.B1.

5 PEDICORD, HARRY WILLIAM. "Restoration Comedy in London."
Restoration, 3 (Fall):66-68.
Notes a 1979 London production of She Wou'd if She Cou'd.

6 STAVES, SUSAN. Players' Scepters: Fictions of Authority in the
Restoration. Lincoln: University of Nebraska Press, passim.
"Studies the changing fictions of authority in late
seventeenth-century England, and shows how secular democratic
myths of authority replaced religious and feudal myths."
Examples used from Etherege's plays.

1980

7 VIETH, DAVID M. "The Discovery of the Date of 'MacFlecknoe.'"
   In Evidence in Literary Scholarship. Essays in Memory of
   James Marshall Osborn. Edited by René Wellek and Alvaro
   Ribeiro. Oxford: Clarendon Press, pp. 63-87.
      In a very long footnote (no. 32 on pp. 74-75), Vieth points
   out plot devices from She Wou'd if She Cou'd also used by
   Shadwell in The Virtuoso (1676). See 1682.B1.

1980

A BOOKS

*1 RIGAUD, N. J. George Etherege: Dramaturge de la Restauration
   anglaise. 2 vols. Lille: Atelier Reproduction des Thèses
   Université de Lille, III; Paris: Diffusion Librarie H.
   Champion, 947 pp.
      Appears to be a reprint of 1976.A2.

B SHORTER WRITINGS

1 BRACHER, FREDERICK. "Etherege at Clement's Inn." Huntington
   Library Quarterly 43:127-34.
      Using legal documents, Bracher describes the life of the
   young law student in 1659-60 and makes conjectures from the
   evidence about Etherege's years at Clement's Inn and possible
   travel to France.

2 BROWN, LAURA S. "The Divided Plot: Tragicomic Form in the Restoration." English Literary History, 47:67-79.
      Concludes her discussion of tragicomic form by comparing
   Etherege's Love in a Tub with Dryden's Marriage A-la-Mode.
   Following the Fletcherian tradition, Restoration tragicomedy
   reconciles "neoclassicism and pragmatism."

3 SCOUTEN, ARTHUR H. and HUME, ROBERT D. "'Restoration Comedy' and
   its Audiences, 1660-1776." Yearbook of English Studies 10:
   45-69.
      A survey of audiences of and for Restoration comedy at
   their original and subsequent productions. Cites the popularity of the plays to show the types in vogue and the changing
   patterns. Notes a decline of interest in Etherege's plays in
   the eighteenth century, and shows that none were picked up
   for revision.

Index

Articles and books are listed alphabetically by title along with the names of the authors. Editions of the plays are given under "Etherege." Not included are titles of anthologies and names of journals. Titles are alphabetical by their first principal word and not by the articles (such as an, the, die, les, etc.) in the title.

Index

The Author in His Work: Essays on a Problem in Criticism, 1978.B7

Baker, David Erskine, 1764.B1; 1782.B1; 1812.B1
Barber, C. L., 1957.B1
Barnard, John, 1971.B1; 1975.B1; 1979.A1
Barnhart, William J., 1955.B1
Barron, Leon O., 1960.B2
Bates, Katherine Lee, 1896.B1
Bateson, F. W., 1951.B1; 1957.B2; 1966.B2; 1972.B1
Bear, Andrew, 1972.B2
"'Beau' Hewyt and John Crowne," 1973.B4
"The *Beau Monde* at the Restoration," 1934.B6
Beless, Rosemary June, 1977.B1
Beljame, Alexandre, 1876.B1; 1881.B1; 1948.B1
Bell, Robert, 1866.B1
Bentley, Eric Russell, 1945.B1
Bentley, Thomas, 1971.B2
Berkeley, David S., 1955.B2, B3; 1959.B1
A Bibliography of the Restoration Drama, 1934.B7
Bigelow, Leslie Platt, 1940.B1
Biographia Britannica, 1750.B2
Biographia Dramatica, or A Companion to the Playhouse, 1782.B1;
    1812.B1
Birdsall, Virginia Ogden, 1967.B1; 1970.B2
Bode, Robert F., 1970.B3
Bond, Donald F., 1965.B7; 1967.B8
Borkat, Roberta F. S., 1976.B1
Boswell, Elenore, 1931.B1
Boyette, P. E., 1966.B3
Bracher, Frederick, 1967.B2, B3; 1969.B1; 1974.A1; 1980.B1
Bratton, Clinton Woodrow, 1975.B2
Brett-Smith, H. F. B., 1927.A1, B1; 1929.B1; 1966.B4; 1971.A1
*A Brief Historical Relation of State Affairs from September 1678 to
    April 1714*, 1857.B2
British Theatre, 1750.B1
"Broadside-Ballad Versions of the Songs in Restoration Drama," 1937.B2
Broich, Ulrich, 1967.B4
Brooke, Stopford, 1876.B2
Brown, Harold Clifford, Jr., 1975.B3
Brown, Laura S., 1980.B2
Bruce, Donald, 1974.B1
Buckingham, George Williers, Duke of, 1705.B1
Burton, K. M. P., 1958.B1
"Bussy-Rabutin et Sir George Etherege," 1961.B1

The Cambridge History of English Literature, 1912.B1
Carnochan, W. B., 1966.A1
Carroll, John Ellison, 1970.B4
"A Case of Restoration: Terry Hands and Timothy O'Brien Talk to R.
    Waterhouse," 1971.B11
Cavalier Drama, 1936.B1

Index

"Contributions to a Dictionary of Critical Terms: I. Comedy of
     Manners," 1951.B1
"The Conventions of Restoration Comedy," 1935.B2
"Conventions of Speech in Restoration Comedy of Manners," 1961.B5
A Conversation between Sir George Etherege and Mr. Fitzjames, 1962.B1
Corder, Jimmie Wayne, 1958.B2
Corman, Brian, 1977.B2
Country Conversations, 1694.B2
Court Satires of the Restoration, 1976.B11
The Court Wits of the Restoration, 1948.B4; 1967.B9
Cox, R. S., Jr., 1968.B5
Crabbed Age and Youth: The Old Men and Women in Restoration Comedy
     of Manners, 1947.B2
Crawford, Bartholow V., 1929.B2
"The Critical Forum: Restoration Comedy Again," 1957.B4
A Critical History of English Literature, 1960.B3
"A Critical Reading of the Comedies of Etherege, Wycherley, and
     Congreve," 1956.B4
"The Critical Reputation of Restoration Comedy in Modern Times,"
     1955.B7
The Critical Reputation of Restoration Comedy of Manners in Modern
     Times up to 1950, 1978.B6
Critical Works
-by John Dennis, 1939.B1
-by Thomas Rymer, 1956.B6
Croissant, DeWitt C., 1935.B1
Cross, Gustav, 1958.B3
"The Cuckold in Restoration Comedy," 1962.B5
Cunningham, John E., 1966.B8

Daiches, David, 1960.B3
Dalldorff, Horst, 1956.B2
"Dame Mary Etherege," 1949.B2
Danchin, Pierre, 1978.B1
Davies, Paul C., 1969.B2; 1972.B3
Davies, Thomas, 1784.B1
De Arte Graphica, 1695.B1; 1962.B2
Deepak, K., 1972.B4
"The Defaced Angel: A Concept of Satanic Grace in Etherege's The Man
     of Mode," 1969.B6
A Defense of Dramatick Poetry, 1698.B1
A Defense of Plays, 1707.B1
A Defence of Sir Fopling Flutter, 1722.B1; 1973.A2
Deitz, Jonathan Eric, 1972.B2
"Delicate and Indelicate Puns in Restoration Comedy," 1966.B5
Dennis, John, 1702.B1; 1722.B1; 1939.B1; 1973.B1
"The Design of Plot: The New Directions of Plot Resolution in late
     Restoration Satiric Comedy," 1972.B5
Despatches of William Perwich, English Agent in Paris, 1669-1677,
     1903.B1

118

The Development of English Drama in the late Seventeenth Century,
    1976.B3
"The Dialect of Those Frantic Times," 1965.B1
Diary
-of John Evelyn, 1664.B1; 1879.B1; 1955.B5
-of Samuel Pepys, 1665.B1; 1666.B1; 1668.B1, B2; 1669.B1; 1893.B1;
    1968.B15
Dibden, Charles, 1800.B1
Dictionary of National Biography, 1885.B2
"The Discovery of the Date of 'MacFlecknoe,'" 1979.B7
A Dissertation on Reading the Classics, 1715.B1
"Diversity and Development in Restoration Comedy, 1660-1679," 1972.B7
"Divided Consciousness: The Trauma and Triumph of Restoration
    Culture," 1977.B9
"The Divided Plot: Tragicomic Form in the Restoration," 1980.B2
The Divine Average: A View of Comedy, 1971.B6
Doran, John, 1864.B2; 1888.B1
Dorimant [pseudonym], 1722.B3
"Dorimant and the Comedy of a Man of Mode," 1969.B4
Downes, John, 1708.B1; 1969.B3
"Drama from the Restoration till 1710," 1971.B1
"The Dramatic Function of Bawdy in the Plays of George Etherege,"
    1978.B5
Dramatic Miscellanies, 1784.B1
"The Dream of Self-Fulfillment in Restoration Comedy: A Study in
    Two Parts: The Heroic Pattern in Aristophanic and Roman Comedy,
    and its Design and Decadence in English Comedy from 1660 to
    1700," 1969.B9
Dryden, John, 1682.B1; 1694.B1; 1695.B1; 1962.B2
Dobrée, Bonamy, 1924.B2; 1925.B1; 1926.B1; 1938.B1; 1946.B1; 1951.B2;
    1955.B4; 1958.B4; 1962.B1; 1967.B5; 1970.B5
Dukore, Bernard F., 1962.A3
Duncan-Jones, E. E., 1971.B5
Dunham, Samuel A., 1838.B1

"The Effect of the Restoration on Drama," 1961.B2
Ellehauge, Martin, 1933.B1; 1974.B2
Elwin, Malcom, 1928.B2; 1966.B9
"The Emergence of Sentimental Comedy, 1660-1707," 1950.B1
Emery, John P., 1966.B10
Eminent Literary and Scientific Men of Great Britain and Ireland,
    1838.B1
"Emotion, Modes of Expression and Effects on Plot in Selected
    Comedies: 1670-1780," 1975.B4
Empson, William, 1957.B4
Engel, Claire-Eliane, 1961.B1
English Comedy, 1929.B4
English Comedy: Its Role and Nature from Chaucer to the Present Day,
    1975.B9
"The English Comic Spirit on the Restoration Stage," 1967.B1
English Criticism, 1972.B10

Index

English Drama, 1914.B2
English Drama: A Working Bibliography, 1896.B1
English Drama of the Restoration and Eighteenth Century (1642-1780),
    1914.B1; 1921.B2; 1923.B2; 1928.B6; 1932.B2; 1968.B14
English Drama, 1660-1800, A Guide to Information Sources, no. 9,
    1976.B4
English Drama to 1710, 1971.B1
England in the Restoration and Early Eighteenth Century, 1972.B11
"English Law and the Materials of Restoration Comedy," 1942.B1
English Literature, 1876.B2
English Literature of the Late Seventeenth Century, 1969.B10
"English New Comedy," 1953.B1
English Restoration Drama: Its Relation to Past English and Past and
    Contemporary French Drama. From Jonson via Molière to Congreve,
    1933.B1; 1974.B2
"English Sources of Restoration Comedy of Manners," 1924.B4
"Entertaining in the Grand Manner," 1930.B3
"Die Entwicklung englischen Restaurationskomödie (1660-1672)," 1961.B6
"Epistle Dedicatory to The Comical Gallant," 1702.B1
An Epistle to Mr. Southerne, 1711.B2; 1721.B1
An Epistle to Sir Richard Steele, on his Play, Call'd The Conscious
    Lovers, 1722.B4
Essays Critical and Historical Dedicated to Lily B. Campbell, 1950.B4
Essays in Biography, 1680-1726, 1925.B1; 1927.B1 (review); 1967.B5
Essays in Dramatic Literature: The Parrott Presentation Volume,
    1935.B1
Essays of Elia, 1823.B1
"Etherege"
-by Thomas Rugge, 1852.B1
-by George Street, 1893.B2
Etherege, George
-Collected Works
--Drama and Poetry
-editions, 1704.A1; 1715.A1; 1723.A1; 1735.A1; 1888.A1; 1975.A3,
    1977.A1
--Dramatic Works
-editions, 1778.A1; 1927.A1; 1971.A1
--Letters
-editions, 1928.A1; 1971.A2; 1974.A1
-separately printed, 1762.A1
--Poetry
-edition, 1963.A1
-selections, 1684.B1; 1685.B1; 1934.B8; 1954.B7
-Individual Works
--An Account of the Rejoycing at the Dyet at Ratisbonne, 1688.A1
--The Comical Revenge; or, Love in a Tub
-separate editions, 1664.A1, A2; 1667.A1; 1669.A1, A2; 1689.A1;
    1690.A1; 1697.A1
-translation
--Russian, 1975.A1
--The Man of Mode; or, Sir Fopling Flutter

-separate editions, 1676.A1; 1684.A1; 1693.A2; 1697.A1; 1711.A1;
    1723.A2; 1725.A1; 1733.A1; 1752.A1, A2; 1768.A1; 1774.A1; 1962.A3;
    1966.A1; 1973.A1; 1979.A1
-in collections and anthologies, 1923.A1; 1929.A1; 1931.A1, A2;
    1932.A1; 1934.A1; 1935.A1; 1938.A1; 1939.A1; 1946.A1; 1953.A1;
    1953.A2; 1955.A1; 1959.A1, A2; 1962.A4; 1962.A5; 1964.A1;
    1966.A2; 1968.A1, A2; 1969.A1; 1970.A1; 1973.A2, A3; 1974.A2;
    1975.A2; 1976.A1; 1978.A1
-scenes from, 1928.A2; 1930.A1
-song from, 1676.A2
-translation,
--French (scenes), 1967.A1
--She Wou'd if She Cou'd
-separate editions, 1668.A1; 1671.A1; 1693.A1; 1710.A1; 1723.A3;
    1972.A1; 1973.A4
-in collections and anthologies, 1970.A2; 1974.A2
-translations,
--Polish, 1962.A2
--Russian (proposed), 1976.B10
"Etherege à la école de Molière," 1968.B1
"Etherege and Cowley," 1927.B4
"Etherege and Holbein," 1954.B6
Etherege and Seventeenth-Century Comedy of Manners, 1957.A1; 1969.A2
"Etherege and the Comic Shallowness," 1975.B3
"Etherege as Diplomat," 1969.B1
"Etherege at Clement's Inn," 1980.B1
"Etherege at Constantinople," 1956.B3
"Etherege, Shadwell, Wycherley, Congreve, Vanbrugh, and Farquhar,"
    1975.B1
"Etherege's Julia," 1947.B3
"Etherege's 'Man of Mode' and Rochester's 'Artermisa to Cloe,'"
    1958.B5
"Etherege's She Would if She Could, I.i.134," 1978.B3
The Ethos of Restoration Comedy, 1971.B8
Evelyn, John, 1664.B1; 1818.B1; 1879.B1; 1955.B5
Evidence in Literary Scholarship: Essays in Memory of James Marshall
    Osborn, 1979.B7
"The Evolution of the Humours Character in Seventeenth-Century English
    Comedy," 1966.B18
An Exact Catalogue of [Plays] . . . Printed . . . till . . . 1680,
    1680.B1
"The Extravagant Rake in Restoration Comedy," 1972.B9

"A Familiar Epistle to Mr. Julian, Secretary of the Muses," 1705.B1
Feddern, Gert-Detlef, 1954.B1
Feltham, Fredrik G., 1951.B3
Felton, Henry, 1715.B1
Fenton, Elijah, 1711.B2; 1721.B1
Ferguson, Thomas Ewing, 1930.B1
Ferrell, David Michael, 1973.B2
"Figurative Structure in Restoration Comedy," 1962.B3

Filmer, Edward, 1707.B1
The First Modern Comedies: The Significance of Etherege, Wycherley,
    and Congreve, 1959.B3; 1967.B6
["The First Play of George Etherege"], 1968.B11
Fitzgerald, Percy, 1882.B1
Flattery, Bruce, 1974.B3
"The Fop and Related Figures in Drama from Jonson to Cibber," 1965.B3
Ford, Dan, 1976.B2
"Foreshadowings of the New Woman in the English Drama of the Seven-
    teenth and early Eighteenth Century," 1950.B3
Forgues, E.-D., 1857.B1
"The Formative Years of Restoration Comedy," 1977.B7
"Das Fortleben des Elisabethanischen Drama im Zeitalter der
    Restauration," 1925.B2
Foster, Dorothy, 1922.B1-4; 1927.B3; 1928.B3, B4; 1932.B1
Fraenatus [pseudonym], 1876.B3
Freehafer, John H., 1950.B1
"French Sources of the Restoration 'Imperfect Enjoyment' Poem,"
    1963.B4
"Frienship in Fashion: The Dramatic Treatment of Friendship in the
    Restoration and Eighteenth Century," 1956.B5
Froberg, Georg, 1925.B2
From Dryden to Johnson, 1957.B3
Fujii, Akio, 1934.B1
Fujimura, Thomas H., 1950.B2; 1952.B1; 1956.B3; 1968.B6; 1973.B3

Gagen, Jean Elisabeth, 1950.B3; 1954.B2; 1978.B2
Gassner, John, 1940.B2; 1945.B2; 1954.B3
The Gay Couple in Restoration Comedy, 1948.B3; 1971.B9
"The Genesis of Steele's 'The Conscious Lovers,'" 1950.B4
Genest, John, 1832.B1
George Etheredge, 1900.A1
"George Etheredge," 1900.B1
"George Etherege," 1921.B3
"George Etherege and his Love in a Tub,: 1974.B7
"George Etherege and the Destiny of Restoration Comedy," 1972.B10
"George Etherege and the Form of a Comedy," 1965.B5; 1966.B17;
    1973.B12
"George Etherege: Dramaturge de la Restauration Anglaise," 1976.A2.
"George Etherege's She Wou'd if She Cou'd," 1976.B10
Germer, Erich, 1963.B2
Geschichte de Englischen Literatur . . . 1660-1700, 1865.B1
Gibb, Carson, 1962.B3
Gildon, Charles, 1699.B1
Gillet, J. E., 1913.B1
"'Give me your Hands': Reflections on the Author's Agent in Comedy,"
    1978.B7
Gladding, Bessie A., 1926.B2
Glide, Joseph M., 1964.B1
Godfrey, Lydia Boker, 1896.B1
The Golden Labrinth: A Study of British Drama, 1962.B4

Goodman, Oscar Bernard, 1953.B1
Gosse, Edmund, 1881.B2; 1883.B1; 1885.B1; 1897.B1; 1910.B2; 1913.B2
Gould, Robert, 1689.B1; 1709.B1
Gratz, David Kenneth, 1975.B4
Great Writers of the English Language: Dramatists, 1979.B3
Grisy, A. de, 1878.B1

Ham, Roswell, G., 1925.B3
Hammond, Anthony, 1973.B4
Hanson, John A., 1974.B4
Harbage, Alfred, 1936.B1
Harris, Bernard, 1965.B1
Hartman, Jay Harry, 1974.B5
Harvey-Jellie, W., 1906.B3
Hatton, Charles, 1878.B2, B3
Hatton Family Correspondence, 1878.B2, B3
Hawkins, Harriet, 1972.B6
Hayman, John Griffiths, 1964.B2; 1968.B7; 1969.B4
Hayward, John, 1930.B2
Hazlitt, William, 1819.B1
Heldt, W., 1922.B5
"Heroes and Heroines in English Comedy, 1660-1750," 1946.B4
Hettner, Herman, 1856.B1
Hewins, Elizabeth L., 1927.B4; 1930.B3
"High Comedy and Low Comedy in England, 1660-1676; A Study in the
    Development of the Comedy of Manners," 1955.B1
"High Comedy in Terms of Restoration Practice," 1929.B2
Hirst, David L., 1979.B1
"His Excellency Sir George Etherege," 1925.B1; 1967.B5
Hiscock, W. G., 1952.B2
Histoire de la Comédie Anglaise au Dix-Septième Siècle: 1672-1707,
    1878.B1
Histoire de literatur du angleterre, 1864.B3
Historical Manuscripts Commission Calendar of the Manuscripts of the
    Marquis of Bath, 1907.B2, B3
A History of English Dramatic Literature to the Death of Queen Anne,
    1875.B1; 1899.B2
History of English Literature, 1871.B1
A History of English Literature, 1927.B2
A History of Restoration Drama, 1923.B3; 1928.B7; 1940.B4; 1952.B4
"Hobbism and Restoration Comedy," 1953.B3
Hogan, Charles Beecher, 1968.B8, B9
Holland, Norman Norwood, Jr., 1956.B4; 1957.B4; 1959.B3; 1967.B6
Holland, Peter, 1979.B2
Hood, Eugene, 1824.B1
Houghton, Walter E., Jr., 1943.B1
Howarth, R. G., 1945.B3
Howling, Robert T., 1954.B4
Hoy, Cyrus, 1961.B2; 1964.B3
Hughes, Leo, 1940.B3
Hume, Robert D., 1972.B7, B8; 1973.B5; 1976.B3; 1977.B3, B4; 1980.B3

Index

"Humor Characterization in Restoration Comedy, 1660-1700," 1973.B9
The Humorists, 1671.B2; 1927.B5
"The Humorists: An Elizabethan Method of Characterization as
    Modified by Etherege and Congreve," 1947.B1
Huseboe, Arthur, 1975.B5, B6; 1978.B3
The Hyacinth Room: An Investigation into the Nature of Comedy,
    Tragedy, and Tragicomedy, 1964.B3
Hymas, Scott Simpson, 1964.B4

The Idea of Honour in the English Drama, 1591-1700, 1951.B1
"Imitation to Emulation: 'Imitation of Nature' from the Restoration
    to the Eighteenth Century," 1978.B8
"The Independent Woman in the Restoration Comedy of Manners," 1975.B7
The Independent Woman in the Restoration Comedy of Manners, 1976.B6
L'Influence Française en Angleterre au XVIIe Siècle: Le Théâtre et
    la Critique, 1906.B2
"The Influence of French Comedy on English Comedy of the late Seven-
    teenth Century," 1899.B1
The Influence of Molière on Restoration Comedy, 1910.B1
"Innocence and Experience as Structural Comic Values in Selected
    Plays of the Restoration and Eighteenth Century," 1975.B10
"Interpreting and Misinterpreting The Man of Mode," 1977.B2
"Introduction to The Dramatic Works of Sir George Etherege," 1927.A1;
    1966.B4; 1971.A1
Isaacs, J., 1921.B1

Jacob, Giles, 1719.B1; 1723.B1
Jansen, Hilde, 1934.B2
Jantz, Ursula, 1978.B4
Jeffares, A. Norman, 1974.A2, A3
"John Evelyn, Jun., as a Literary Critic," 1952.B2
"John Wilmot, Comte de Rochester," 1857.B1
Johnson, Frank L., 1935.B2
Jones, Stephen, 1812.B1
Jordan, R. J., 1965.B2; 1972.B9
Juvenalis Redivivus, 1683.B1

Kaul, A.N., 1970.B6
Kavenik, Frances Mary-Michele, 1977.B5
Kerby, W. Mosley, 1907.B1
Kiley, Frederick, 1968.B10
Killigrew, Thomas, 1720.B1
Kirkman, Francis, 1671.B1
Kishi, Tetsuo, 1968.B10; 1972.B10
Knight, G. Wilson, 1962.B4
Knights, L. C., 1937.B1; 1946.B2; 1964.B5; 1966.B11; 1973.B6
Koonce, Howard Lee, 1969.B5
Kornbluth, Martin Leonard, 1956.B5
Krause, David, 1969.B6
Kreutz, Irving, 1970.B7
Kronenberger, Louis, 1952.B3

Krutch, Joseph Wood, 1924.B3; 1949.B1; 1961.B3; 1969.B7

Lacedemonian Mercury, 1692.B1
Lacey, T. A., 1928.B5
Lamb, Charles, 1822.B1; 1823.B1; 1973.B7
"Lamb and Restoration Comedy," 1979.B4
"Lamb's Criticism of Restoration Comedy," 1943.B1
Lamson, Roy, Jr., 1937.B2
Langbaine, Gerard, 1680.B1; 1688.B1, B2; 1691.B1; 1971.B3
Langhans, Edward A., 1973.B8
"The Language of Eros in Restoration Comedy," 1974.B4
"L. C. Knights and Restoration Comedy," 1966.B2; see also 1957.B2
Lectures on the English Comic Writers, 1819.B1
Leech, Clifford, 1951.B4
Legouis, P., 1966.B12; 1968.B12; 1971.B5
Leon, Edelma de, 1978.B5
"Letter of 17 Nov.," 1812.B3
"Letter to John Wilmot, Earl of Rochester," 1907.B2
"Letter to the Earl of Rochester," 1907.B3; 1941.B1
The Letters of Saint-Evremond, 1930.B2
Letters to his Friends, 1779.B1
"The Letterbooks of Sir George Etherege," 1967.B2
Lewis, Mineko S., 1973.B9
"Libertin und Heroischer Held: Das Drama der Englischen Restauration-
    zeit und Seine Leitbilder," 1967.B4
"Libertine and Précieux Elements in Restoration Comedy," 1959.B2
"The Libertine Gentleman in Restoration Comedy," 1965.B2
Lightfoot, John Ewell, Jr., 1973.B10
Likenesses of Truth in Elizabethan and Restoration Drama, 1972.B6
"The Limits of Historical Veracity in Neoclassic Drama," 1972.B11
Link, Frederick M., 1976.B4
A Literary History of England, 1948.B2; 1967.B8
Literary Remains, 1836.B1
"Literature No 'Document,'" 1924.B5
Lives and Characters of the English Dramatick Poets, 1699.B1
Lives of the Most Famous English Poets, 1687.B1
Lives of the Norths, 1826.B1
Lives of the Poets of Great Britain and Ireland, 1753.B1
Lives of the Rakes, 1924.B1
Lockwood, Thomas, 1969.B8
Loftis, John, 1950.B4; 1966.B13; 1969.B3; 1972.B11
London Gazette, 1676.B1
The London Stage, 1660-1800, 1960.B1; 1961.B4; 1962.B7; 1965.B9;
    1968.B8
The London Stage, 1660-1800: A Critical Introduction, 1968.B2, B3,
    B9, B16, B17
Longueville, Thomas, 1902.B1
Lord, George De Forest, 1963.B3
Lott, James David, 1967.B7
Love, Harold H. R., 1964.B6; 1968.B13; 1971.B4; 1972.B2, B9
Luttrell, Narsissis, 1857.B2
Lynch, Kathleen M., 1924.B4; 1926.B3

Index

Macaulay, Thomas Babbington, 1841.B1; 1898.B1
"MacFlecknoe," 1682.B1
MacLeod, William R., 1934.B3
McAfee, H., 1916.B1
McCamic, Frances Smith, 1931.A3; 1974.A4
McCollum, William G., 1971.B6
McDonald, Charles O., 1964.B7
McDonald, Margaret Lamb, 1975.B7; 1976.B6
McDowell, Margaret Blaine, 1954.B5
McMillin, Scott, 1973.A2
Malek, James S., 1979.B3
"The Man of Mode and The Plain Dealer: Common Origins and Parallels,"
    1966.B1
"[The Man of Mode as a Comedy of Wit]," 1973.B3
Mandach, André de, 1946.B3
"Margery Pinchwife's 'London Disease': Restoration Comedy in the
    Libertine Offensive of the 1670's," 1977.B6
"Marital Discord in English Comedy from Dryden to Fielding," 1977.B3
"Marriage of Convenience and the Moral Code of Restoration Comedy,"
    1962.B8
Marshall, Julian, 1888.B2
Martin, Leslie H., 1976.B5
Marvell, Andrew, 1676.B2; 1968.B12; 1971.B5
"Masking and Disguise in the Plays of Etherege, Wycherley, and
    Congreve," 1970.B4
Masters of the Drama, 1940.B2; 1945.B2; 1954.B3
Matalene, Henry William, III, 1970.B8
Matrimonial Law and the Materials of Restoration Comedy, 1942.B2
The Matrons: Six Short Histories, 1762.A1
Maurocordato, A., 1967.A1
Meindl, Vincenz, 1901.A1; 1964.A2
Memoirs
-by John Evelyn, 1818.B1
-by Samuel Pepys, 1825.B1
Men of Letters and the English Public in the Eighteenth Century,
    1660-1744, 1948.B1
Mignon, Elizabeth, 1943.B2; 1947.B2
Miles, Dudley Howe, 1910.B1; 1916.B2
Miner, Earl R., 1966.B14; 1972.B10; 1974.B6
Minor, Charles B., 1957.B5
"Mirrors on the Restoration Stage," 1962.B6
Miscellanea Aurea: or the Golden Medley, 1720.B1
MLA Seminar on The Man of Mode, 28 December, 1976, 1976.B7
Mohanty, Harendra Prasad, 1966.B15
Molière and Restoration Comedy in England, 1907.B1
Molière en Angleterre, 1660-1700, 1913.B1
Molière et la Comédie de Moeurs en Angleterre (1660-1668), 1946.B3
Momus Triumphans: or the Plagiaries of the English Stage, 1688.B1;
    1971.B3
"Money: God and King; Economic Aspects of Restoration Comedy,"
    1971.B2

Index

Paine, Clarence, 1940.B5
Palmer, John, 1913.B3; 1973.B11
"Der Parallelismus als Heimsches Stilelement in der Prosadiktion und
    Komposition der Englischen Restaurationskomödie," 1954.B1
Park, Roy, 1979.B4
"Past and Parody in The Man of Mode," 1976.B5
Pedicord, Harry William, 1979.B5
Peltz, Catharine Walsh, 1944.B1
Pepys on the Restoration Stage, 1916.B1
Pepys, Samuel, 1665.B1; 1666.B1; 1668.B1, B2; 1669.B1; 1825.B1;
    1893.B1; 1916.B1; 1935.B3; 1968.B15
Perkinson, Richard H., 1936.B3
Perry, Henry Ten Eyck, 1925.B4
Persson, Agnes Valkay, 1970.B10; 1975.B8
Perwich, William, 1903.B1
Peterson, William M., 1962.B6
Pfitzner, Kaethe, 1931.B2
Phillips, Edward, 1675.B1
Pinto, Vivian de Sola, 1928.B8; 1954.B7; 1965.B4
Pirages, Philip Joe, 1977.B7
Players' Scepters: Fictions of Authority in the Restoration, 1979.B6
The Playgoer's Handbook to Restoration Drama, 1928.B2; 1966.B9
"The Play-house, a Satyr," 1709.B1
The Playhouse of Pepys, 1935.B3
"The Plays of Sir George Etherege: A Production-Oriented Approach,"
    1968.A3
Poems [by R. Gould], 1689.B1
Poems and Letters [of Andrew Marvell], 1971.B5
Poems on Affairs of State, 1697.B1; 1963.B3
Poems on Several Occasions [by Rochester], 1680.B2; see also 1959.B5
Poeta de Tristibus, 1968.B11; 1971.B4
"The Poetic Romp," 1963.B1
The Poetical Register, 1719.B1; 1723.B1
Porte, Michael Sheldon, 1960.B4
Potter, L. D., 1965.B3
Powell, Jocelyn, 1965.B5; 1966.B17; 1973.B12
The Précieuse, or Distressed Heroine of Restoration Comedy, 1959.B1
"Préciosité and the Restoration Comedy of Manners," 1955.B2
"Preface of the Translator to 'A Parallel betwixt Painting and
    Poetry,'" 1962.B2; see also, 1695.B1
A Preface to Restoration Drama, 1965.B10; 1968.B18
Preliminary Essays, 1957.B7
Price, Stanley, 1971.B7
"Pride of Reason in the Restoration," 1959.B4
Prideaux, W. F., 1898.B2
The Prologues and Epilogues of the Restoration (1660-1700): A
    Tentative Check-List, 1978.B1
"A Prompt Copy of Etherege's Man of Mode," 1968.B4
Le public et les hommes de lettres en Angleterre au XVIIIe siècle
    (1660-1744), 1881.B1; 1948.B1

Quaintance, Richard E., 1963.B4
"The Quality of Wit in Comedies of Etherege, Wycherley, Congreve,
    and Shadwell," 1951.B3
"The Quest for the Good Society, Friends and Family," 1960.B2

R. E. R., 1812.B3
Radcliffe, Alexander, 1682.B2
"Raillery during the Restoration Period and Early Eighteenth Century,"
    1964.B2
"Raillery in Restoration Comedy," 1966.B7
"Raillery in Restoration Satire," 1968.B7
"Rakes and Fools: A Study of the Development of the Libertine-
    Satiric Tradition in Restoration Comedy, 1660-1676," 1964.B1
"The Rake's Progress from Court to Comedy: A Study in Comic Form,"
    1966.B21
The Ramble, 1682.B2
Ray, Jimmie Karen Couch, 1977.B8
"Reading and Misreading The Man of Mode," 1972.B8
"The Reception of Restoration Comedy of Manners in Nineteenth-
    Century England: An Account of Wycherley, Congreve, Vanbrugh,
    and Farquhar on the Stage and in the Study," 1972.B12
Records of the Scots Colleges at Douai, Rome, Madrid, Valladolid, and
    Ratisbon, 1906.B1
Reed, Isaac, 1782.B1; 1812.B1
"Reflections of the Law in the Comedies of Etherege, Wycherley, and
    Congreve," 1977.B1
"The Relation of Molière to Restoration Comedy," 1931.B3
The Relation of Molière to Restoration Comedy, 1938.B2; 1964.B8
"Renaissance and Restoration Perspectives on the Experience of
    Comedy," 1974.B3
Restoration and Eighteenth-Century Comedy, 1973.A2
Restoration Carnival, 1954.B7
"Restoration Comedy," 1957.B3
Restoration Comedy, 1974.A2, A3
"Restoration Comedy: A Revaluation," 1966.B15
"'Restoration Comedy' and its Audiences, 1660-1776," 1980.B3
"Restoration Comedy and its Modern Critics," 1956.B8; 1957.B7
"Restoration Comedy and Later," 1955.B6
"Restoration Comedy and the Critics," 1963.B5
"Restoration Comedy and the Provok'd Critics," 1972.B2
"Restoration Comedy as Drama of Satire: An Investigation into
    Seventeenth-Century Aesthetics," 1964.B7
"Restoration Comedy in London," 1979.B5
The Restoration Comedy of Wit, 1952.B1; 1968.B6
"Restoration Comedy (Reconsiderations II)," 1945.B5
"Restoration Comedy Re-examined," 1972.B13
Restoration Comedy, 1660-1720, 1924.B2; 1938.B1; 1946.B4; 1951.B2;
    1955.B4; 1958.B4; 1962.B1; 1970.B5
"Restoration Comedy: The Critical View, 1913-1965," 1967.B7
"Restoration Comedy: The Earlier Phase," 1951.B4
"Restoration Comedy: The Reality and the Myth," 1937.B1; 1946.B2;

Scott, Virgil J., 1945.B4
"Scottish Religious Houses Abroad," 1864.B1
Scouten, Arthur H., 1961.B4; 1966.B19; 1968.B2, B16; 1976.B9; 1980.B3
"The Second Letterbook of Sir George Etherege," 1952.B5
"Second Thoughts: II. L. C. Knights and Restoration Comedy," 1957.B2;
    1966.B2; 1972.B1
"Sentimentale Züge in den Lustspielgesalten Ethereges, Wycherleys,
    Congreves, Vanbrughs, and Farquhars," 1963.B2
"The Servant in Restoration Comedy," 1960.B4
"The Session of Poets," 1697.B1
Settle, Elkanah, 1698.B1
Seventeenth-Century Studies, 1883.B1; 1885.B1; 1897.B1; 1913.B2
"The Seventeenth-Century Wit and Fop: A Study of Restoration Comedy
    in its Relation to the Life of Fashion," 1930.B1
Shadwell, Thomas, 1671.B2; 1927.B5
Shakespeare Studies: Historical and Comparative in Method, 1927.B6;
    1942.B3
Sharma, Ram Chandra, 1961.B5; 1965.B6
Sheffield, John, Marquis of Normanby, 1695.B2; 1701.B1; 1702.B2;
    1716.B1
Sherbo, Arthur, 1949.B3, B4
Sherburn, George, 1948.B2; 1967.B8
"A Short Defense . . .," 1722.B2
A Short View of Tragedy, 1963.B1; 1956.B6
Simon, Irene, 1959.B4; 1963.B5
Singh, S., 1953.B2
Singh, Sarup, 1963.B6
"Sir George Etheredge," 1898.B2
"Sir George Etheredge: A Neglected Chapter of English Literature,"
    1881.B2
Sir George Etheredge, Sein Leben, Seine Seit und Seine Dramen,
    1901.A1; 1964.A2
"Sir George Etherege"
-Anon., 1928.B1
-by Boswell, 1931.B1
-by Foster, 1928.B4; 1932.B1
-by Fujii, 1934.B1
-by Gosse, 1910.B2
-by Scouten, 1976.B9
-by Swaen, 1922.B6
-by Wainewright, 1926.B4
"Sir George Etherege, I," 1922.B3
"Sir George Etherege, II," 1922.B4
"Sir George Etherege (1636-1689), 1876.B1, B3
Sir George Etherege: A Study in Restoration Comedy (1660-1680),
    1931.A3; 1974.A4
"Sir George Etherege and his Secretary," 1967.B3
"Sir George Etherege and the Restoration 'Code Hero,'" 1968.B10
"Sir George Etherege: Collections," 1927.B3
"Sir George Etherege: Collections: Addenda," 1928.B3
"Sir George Etherege and his Guilded Butterflies," 1927.B7

Van Der Weele, Steven John, 1955.B7; 1978.B6
Van Lennep, William, 1965.B9
"The Velvet Vizard: The Ethic of Dissimulation in Restoration
    Comedy," 1977.B8
Verity, A. W., 1888.A1; 1893.B3; 1975.A3; 1977.A1
Vernon, Paul F., 1962.B8
Victor, Benjamin, 1722.B4
Vieth, David M., 1958.B5; 1959.B5; 1977.B9; 1979.B7
"The Views of Mr. Symons," 1945.B1
"The Virtuous Women in the Restoration Play-World: The Concept of
    Marriage and the Social Status of Women in the Comedies of
    Etherege, Wycherley, and Congreve," 1977.B10
"Les Voies de la Critique Récente: Comment elle étudie la comédie
    de la Restauration," 1966.B12
"Vows, Prayers, and Dice: Comic Values in The Man of Mode," 1976.B1

Wain, John, 1956.B8; 1957.B7
Wainewright, John B., 1921.B3; 1926.B4
Waith, Eugene, 1968.A1; 1971.B10; 1978.B7
Wall, Donald Clark, 1963.B8
Walpole, Horace, 1798.B1
Ward, Adolphus William, 1875.B1; 1899.B2
Waterhouse, R., 1971.B11
Weiss, Adolf, 1924.B6
Weiss, Samuel Abba, 1953.B3
"Die Welt der Restaurationskomödie: Ein Querschnitt druch die
    Lustspiele Hauptsächlich von Etherege, Wycherley, und Congreve
    zur Erfassung ihrer Stofflichen Wesenszüge," 1956.B2
Wertheim, Albert, 1980.B4
Whincop, Thomas, 1749.B1
"Who's Holding the Mirror?", 1970.B7
"The Widow of Ephesus: Some Reflections on an International Comic
    Theme," 1956.B7
Wilcox, John, 1931.B3; 1938.B2; 1964.B8
Wild Civility: The English Comic Spirit on the Restoration Stage,
    1970.B2
Wilkinson, D. R. M., 1964.B9
Williams, Basil, 1928.B12
Williamson, George, 1927.B7
Wilson, John Harold, 1939.B2; 1947.B3; 1948.B4; 1965.B10; 1967.B9;
    1968.B18; 1976.B11
Winstanley, William, 1687.B1
Wood, Thomas, 1683.B1
Works
-by Buckingham, 1705.B1
-by Gould, 1709.B1
-by Macaulay, 1898.B1
-by Shadwell, 1927.B5
-by Walpole, 1798.B1
"The Works of Etherege," 1929.B1
Wright, James, 1694.B2
Würzbach, Wolfgang, 1900.B1